Frenchie

Jacqueline Jourdan

the Peppertree Press
Sarasota, Florida

For information regarding permission,
call 941-922-2662 or contact us at our website:
www.peppertreepublishing.com or write to:
the Peppertree Press, LLC.
Attention: Publisher
1269 First Street, Suite 7
Sarasota, Florida 34236

ISBN: 978-1-936343-76-8

Library of Congress Number: 2011924499

Printed in the U.S.A.

Printed May 2011

Dedication

*I dedicate this book to my dear children and grandchildren with
great love and an abundant definition of Life, a Magnificent Bitch.
If only I had understood its splendor when I was young,
instead of concentrating on its disappointments.*

*Life is a constant battle, but so well worth the fight.
Life offers us the magnificent beauty of nature.
The magic of love with its heartrending thrills and sorrows.*

*What Happy Pills can compare with what God has given us?
The wonder of it all … its sumptuous pleasures and agonizing
tragedies. Yes, Life, my dearest ones, is a Magnificent Bitch.*

Frenchie

I was born in Paris, France. When I was about four years old, I recall being very ill, burning with fever. I remember a large tub of water next to my bed. My father was arguing with a woman dressed in white. She was the doctor and they were arguing about the doctor placing me into the tub of cold water to get my fever down.

My mother was standing aside with her head bent down softly crying. I was blacking out, so I don't remember everything. Years later, I was told that my father was so enraged, he pushed the doctor down the stairs, but she was not really hurt. Like most people of his generation, he believed the fever should be treated with heat, closed windows and a steaming room.

I was then given the treatments of ventouse and cataplasm, which consisted of barbaric, but fairly efficient medications or remedies as we called it. The ventouse treatment consisted of a thick heavy glass that a ball of cotton was placed inside and then saturated with alcohol, ignited, and applied to the back. In worse cases like pneumonia, to draw water from the lungs, they would make small incisions in the skin with a sharp knife. Then they applied the lighted ventouse directly to the lungs to draw as much liquid as possible from the infected lungs. In my case, I had double pneumonia, which didn't make it easy. The other treatment of cataplasm consisted of some mustard concoction, heated to a boiling point, put into cheesecloth and applied immediately to your back. Hot! Hot! Hot! Never a lobster turned redder than the skin of your back. Some of your skin comes up with the cataplasm when it was lifted from your back.

I was also plagued with ear infections and that *treatment* was by far my worst nightmare. Oil was heated to the limit I was able to stand and then poured into my ear. God, I hated that!

Sore throats were cured, or hoped to be, by having a brush dumped into a God-awful liquid called, *Bleu de Méthylène.* Then they would paint your throat with it making you gag for hours. The remedies, although primitive, worked most of the time and since that was all we had, it was either sink or swim—penicillin was a long way off in the distant future.

After my near death experience of double pneumonia, almost six months had passed. During the time I was in bed, I developed chicken pox and measles, and some other illnesses in between. My Shirley Temple blonde curly locks had to be shaved off, because it was so difficult to comb.

When I finally recovered, my mother called it a miracle—the first of many miracles in my life.

Due to my many illnesses, I developed a phobia, catching colds. Whenever I caught a cold or developed a bronchial infection, these symptoms would send me into an uncontrollable fear, heavy sweating, shortness of breath and a rapid heartbeat. The thought of getting the same respiratory failure I had experienced during my illness would trigger a quiet hysteria within me. Professional help would have been necessary, but in those days, such problems were considered shameful and *strong* people should be able to deal with it themselves. I was too embarrassed to share my *weakness* with someone else and preferred keeping my private hell to myself. As the years went by, I learned to cope with my phobia by trying to avoid colds as much as possible. I would often get friendly teasing from my friends when someone sneezed and I would quickly back up and cover my nose.

When I was quite young, we moved to a very large castle with beautiful lawns, trees (magnificent weeping willow trees), lovely flowers all over and a pond that always had green algae on top. When I was five years old, I remember my governess would walk me down to the pond area and tell me if I got too close, a monster would materialize in the water and pull me in.

Also, she told of a horse and rider whom the monster had pulled in when he had ventured too close. Therefore, if you stood near the pond in the moonlight, the horse and rider would come out of the water and take you in. Needless to say, it scared me to death and kept me from ever going near the pond any time of the day or night.

The castle had four floors—the first floor had a large entrance hall and beautiful Italian marble floors. There was a large staircase leading from the foyer to the upper floors. The second floor was for the master's sleeping quarters and my room was way down at the end of the hallway. The third floor had guest suites and the fourth floor held the servants' quarters. We had quite a staff of servants and I had my own governess and maid.

I was never mistreated, but I still was a very lonely and melancholy child. My parents were busy with their businesses and social calendar. I had a cow named Blanche that followed me around much like a puppy. I played with my dolls and developed quite an imagination to compensate for my loneliness. I remember seeing myself as a merchant, selling many beautiful flowers, which I dearly loved, and changing coins with my customers.

I vividly remember two very traumatic occurrences during my childhood. The first was during a beautiful lawn party at the castle. There was a large table where the guests were seated, with my father at the head of the table and my mother seated at the other end. There were many bottles drunk and much laughter. The servants brought out large trays of food and everyone was having a merry time, including Monsieur LeCure', the Priest. He loved his spirits and his nose and cheeks would turn red. Even though my father was Jewish, he enjoyed the company of Monsieur LeCure'. My father jokingly said he thought Monsieur LeCure' became a priest so he could imbibe without feeling guilty, because he enjoyed wine so much. Monsieur LeCure' was complaining, because he suspected his congregation was putting buttons instead of coins into the offering basket. He said the congregants would "burn in hell for that." His hat would bounce precariously back and forth on his head causing much laughter and teasing. He was much loved by everyone.

I remember someone proposed a toast and everyone stood up with their glasses raised. I was drinking *boisson* (apple juice), not cider, which was alcoholic. Then my governess, whom I addressed as Mademoiselle, told me it was time for us to leave the party and I was pleading my case for staying a bit longer, because I was busy playing with my doll. Mademoiselle took a final drink from her glass of apple cider. Suddenly everything got very quiet. I looked up and saw that everyone was perfectly still … something was terribly wrong. All their eyes focused on my governess who was gasping for air and making gurgling sounds. I remember I was holding her apron and frantically calling her name.

When someone in the group mentioned the word bee, everyone began shouting like wildfire. She was turning purple and fell back into Monsieur LeCure's arms. I was hysterical by then, holding onto her arm and calling her name. Someone finally pulled me away and carried me screaming and fighting into the castle. Later that day they told me I would never see Mademoiselle again. A bee had fallen into her cider and when she took a drink, it bit her throat and she died.

Things were never quite the same after that. I guess when confronted for the first time with the death of someone who is very close to you, a child loses the sense of security that comes with innocence. I began to have problems with my nerves and my stomach. My parents were often in Paris socializing and I spent most of my time with my grandmother and my maternal uncle. I missed my mother very much.

A new governess from Germany came on the scene. She flirted with my father and thought if she could get rid of me, my father would be willing to leave my mother and marry her. One day she put me into the stroller and pushed me into the street, leaving me alone in hopes that a car would run over me. Of course, my mother fired her immediately. My Father wanted to kill her.

My parents began arguing more frequently and boisterously than usual. I hated those stupid arguments and couldn't understand why if my parents really loved me as much as they said they did, they would not see how sad it made me and stop.

The second traumatic incident I remember vividly. I was playing on the front lawn with my dolls while my parents were having drinks on the patio. Their voices were getting higher and louder. I held my doll very tightly hoping they would stop, but instead the argument escalated to the point they began throwing things at each other. I was crying and pleading for them to stop. I came forward with my arms extended in a plea and didn't see the glass my father had thrown. It crashed into my thumb cutting it in two. I only remember the look of horror on my parents' faces when they picked me up and tried to console my hurt.

I was eight years old when my mother divorced my father. It had become downhill for both of them. My father surrounded himself with his friends: literary and artistic greats of that period such as Picasso, Roland Dorgeles and also Guillaume Apollinaire (who was madly in love with my father's sister, Linda, and for whom he wrote many poems) and, of course, women, always more women.

My Mother had her music. Although gifted with a beautifully well-trained operatic voice, she could never bring herself to face an audience. She was a big disappointment to my father, who had spent a fortune on teachers in hopes that she would sing at the Paris Opera House. It seems some men need the glamour of a woman in show business to flatter their ego. I found that out later on in my own life. I don't know if that was one of the elements that triggered the breakup of their marriage or not. With all due respect and love for my mother, she was not the most ambitious person in the world—a little weak and shy. In all fairness, my father with his endless string of mistresses was probably more than she could endure.

After their breakup, I remember my father coming to pick me up and taking me to Zoos and Fairs, but never alone. He always had some woman, never the same one, at his side and I resented it terribly. I wanted so much to be alone with him and never could understand why he needed anyone else with us—wasn't I enough? Was I such a bore? I loved his company, because he was so much more fun than my mother. I was too young to understand that womanizing, like alcohol and gambling, is an addiction. His love for me was real, but his weakness always followed him.

My father was quite ambitious and brilliant. He owned his own bank and a newspaper, "Paillasse." He was not very tall at 5'5", but nonetheless quite good-looking and charming. My father was eighteen years older than my mother. My mother was taller than he was, with dark hair, blue eyes and beautiful.

This had not been my father's first marriage. He was previously married to one of the Rothchild daughters, I was told, whom he divorced ten years prior to marrying my mother. They had no children.

Both in the past and now, for a woman to have a womanizer for a husband is the utmost hurtful insult— worse even than having a drunkard or a gambler as it greatly lowers the wife's self-esteem. It causes her to lose her self-confidence as a woman, especially having to cope with inquiries from both sides of the family, friends and acquaintances.

Another of my childhood memories is when my Godmother, Charmaine, left my Godfather. He kept playing the song, "Charmaine, Charmaine, will you come back again" while crying into his Pernod. I still like that song.

I remember my father had quite a sense of humor and

was a practical joker. He loved nothing better than playing tricks on people. My father tells this story about Picasso's famous painting of the donkey. "My father, with the help of Dorgeles and Apollinaire, who were the actual artists, took turns dunking the donkey's tail into different color paints, and letting the donkey wiggle its tail all over the canvas. As we know, it became a sensational painting.

The next story was told by my uncle, who used to crack up every time he told it. It went this way: there was a woman named Capucine, an acquaintance, more or less, of the family. She was a little simple-minded and had a major crush on my father. The poor thing was quite homely and Show Biz struck! Neither my father or my mother or any of their friends could discourage her from coming to our home and making eyes at my father, begging him to introduce her to important people in show business.

My father had a friend, a famous impresario who, like my father, loved to play tricks on people and had played a few on my father in the past. One special day, my father had a plan to get even with him. He called Capucine over and mentioned a great part for her in the theater, but he added, "You have to audition for it. "You see," he went on, "you have to wear a religious costume, preferably a nun's and as you force your way into Legrand's office, who by the way is madly in love with you, ignore the receptionist. Just go into his office, stand in front of his desk, jump three times, turn around, bend, lift up your robe and pass gas while shouting, 'I love you.' The more you pass gas, the more your chances are to get the part. But don't forget to shout 'I love you' each time you pass gas. Now don't worry if he asks you to leave, it is his way of testing your talent and perseverance. Then just jump on his lap and kiss him."

Thrilled, the lady proceeded to do as told, wearing her designated outfit and ignoring the receptionist, she crashed into his office and proceeded to do all she had been told, while a stupefied and outraged impresario screamed at her to leave. She jumped on his knees, kissed him and, as the unexpected often happens, probably from emotion, certainly not in the script, she promptly proceeded to relieve herself all over the hysterically disgusted impresario.

Well, the story spread like wild fire and became the joke of not only their inner circle, but all over Paris as well. Mr. Legrand vowed to revenge himself, but of course, could never duplicate that scenario. As for Capucine, she finally learned the truth and became happily married to a butcher. Today such a joke would be considered a 'no-no,' making fun of a not too bright woman. But back then, humor was different, seen without malice. We could laugh with each other and at each other, without being offended. However, for every joke played on women by men, they were duplicated by women on men. People didn't take themselves too seriously in those days. None of the huge paranoia of today existed then.

Around that time, my Uncle Jean was introduced to a pretty girl who was a deaf mute. Again, my father introduced them and encouraged the issue. The girl became pregnant. My uncle married her, but they never lived together. My uncle always implied my father was the one who made her pregnant … and perhaps he was.

This is my uncle's story: "After a year of being apart and without the slightest intimacy, one day she came to my home. She had been sent by her 'crazy' mother and in connivance with your father. She played up to me with sign language and being a man and young (double-whammy), another kid was fabricated. That one was a deaf mute like her mother. I then, promptly got a divorce and saw the boys three times in my life." (Which wasn't much to say on his behalf.)

My uncle eventually ended up with an opera singer, named Suzanne. She had been a kept woman, quite shrewd and older than he was by fifteen years. Despite all his faults, I loved my uncle very much and loved going to his optical store where I was always sure to get a few francs in spite of my *aunt's* objection that he was spoiling me.

I never liked the woman and am sure the feeling was mutual. She was very suspicious of everyone, especially me. She kept changing maids under the pretext of *suspicion of theft* but none was ever proven. Her family consisted of a mother, brother, a nephew, and a niece who couldn't wait to inherit her aunt's goodies. But in all fairness, his wife helped my uncle build his chain of optique and underwater equipment companies in the south of France. His work was all that mattered to him.

Before his strange first marriage, he had deeply loved a lovely young girl. He had known Suzy since childhood and they were engaged. She tragically died of tuberculosis at the age of 20. She was buried with her engagement ring. He never stopped loving her.

As I recall, my father had always been afraid of water and did not let me near the water at the beach. Yet one day after one of his fancy dinner parties with his latest paramour, she insisted they take a rowboat for a ride on the Seine. After all, it was a beautiful day. He reluctantly agreed and the rest is debatable. It seems the boat tilted after one of them stood up. My father fell overboard. Although the ambulance came immediately, my father, possibly from fear had a stroke and died. I was 10 years old. I loved him very much, and to this day, it is a great loss. Melancholy as well as anxiety became a great part of my life, which I have had to fight all my life.

A new man had come into my mother's life. He was an aristocrat, Count F de Rieux, a French nobleman from way back. His medieval castle still stands in Rouen in Normandy.

He was a disciplinarian and as it turned out, he was also a womanizer, but she was crazy about him.

When I was about eight and a half years old, we moved with him to Rouen, Normandy. He came from a very rich family and his endowed mother was his benefactor, as he never worked a day in his life.

It is always difficult for a child to understand an adult's actions, change in environment, new parents, new authority, and the unfairness of being with someone who has no business being around children. My new stepfather was a cold, sadistic aristocrat who still lived in the middle ages and believed that children "should not be seen nor heard" and for whom punishment should be frequent, whether deserved or not. His favorite punishment was spanking my bare behind with a hard bristle brush until blood came out.

I almost always had my meals with my maid. When I was allowed to eat at the adult's table, I almost invariably ended up standing in the corner of the room until my stepfather decided it was enough, which usually lasted one hour—no talking, nor moving. I almost always got in trouble when I tried to speak at the table or for not sitting straight without my hands on the table. Food was my biggest enemy, especially èndives braisées. God, how I hated them! They made me gag and I can still taste them to this day. Even throwing up made me end up in the corner of the room.

From the very beginning, I rebelled against his tyrannical ways and for taking my father's place. It became a constant unspoken war between the two of us. He was never able to break me and that infuriated him. As I grew older, it became evident to me that it excited his sick sadistic mind. It was a strange sort of life, with my mother trying to please him and me trying to displease him, which he invariably blamed on my Jewish background.

His strong royalist upbringing didn't help matters much. He was the master of all he surveyed—every domestic from maid to cook weren't employed unless he approved them. They were almost always bashful young country girls and didn't stay in our service more than four to six months.

They were either pregnant or *unsatisfactory* workers, which meant their chances for a new job were very small if not nil.

Our old dog, Mascot, was probably worse off than any of us. Half-blind and arthritic, the poor old gal could not respond to F de Rieux's command fast enough and therefore had to endure leather strap beatings.

I remember one day, I must have been nine. I was playing in the house when my stepfather's loud voice and Mascot's cries got to me. As I stepped into the garden, my stepfather was standing with the leather strap or *martinet*, which he usually used on me—but this time, the dog was his victim. The poor old beast was on her side, her head tilted as if begging him to stop. My mother was there mildly objecting. My grandmother, who was visiting, was crying and asking him to stop. My young nine-year-old mind took only a few seconds to grasp the whole situation. As rage set in, I raced toward my beloved dog and grabbed the martinet from his hand and lashed at him in the face. A cold silence followed as I bent over my trembling dog and picked him up. By then, the servants were all standing there looking, silently enjoying my guts. "I'll deal with you later," hissed my stepfather at me while chasing the domestics away with his hand. He then walked away holding the cheek where the martinet had hit, ignoring my mother and grandmother who were trying to make excuses for me. My poor Mascot died two months after that.

From that moment on, we really hated each other. He never missed a chance to punish me and I never failed to annoy him. Many times, I felt the martinet and the brush on my behind. If the punishments were not corporal, they were psychological.

I had a pet duck named Alfred who followed me everywhere and quacked with delight at the sight of me. Many times, he would try to follow on the country road to school. My maid would take him back under her arm regardless of many quack, quacks of protest.

My stepfather hated that duck and the duck hated him for good reason. He delighted in scaring the poor bird by chasing him away with a stick or making loud noises. Alfred would try unsuccessfully to fly away, but would always end up in the bushes, minus a few feathers. One morning while I was still in bed, I heard a commotion coming from the garden. Still half asleep, I stumbled out of bed and rushed to the window. My duck was lying there in the driveway, a mess of blood and feathers. My stepfather had run his car over him. He swore that it was an *accident*, but the smirk on his face told me the truth.

We went to live in Rouen, Neufchatel, since our château had been sold and he bought this house. It was a typical Normand style. Its brown and beige pillars intertwined, which gave it a cheerful and warm look. The garden wasn't large compared to our château, and a big old tree with its enormous trunk and weeping willow branches gave the garden a haunted look and atmosphere. A stone balcony also added to a medieval atmosphere. Two enormous wooden doors gave entrance from the street and access to a large garage. To the right, hidden by large trees stood our home. Inside was the typical "Normand" style with its big kitchen, an enormous assortment of pots and pans in cuivre (copper). The stove shone brilliantly and one of the servants was assigned the job to polish all this once a week, a job that took more than a day. *Confiture* (jam) was made in one of the biggest pots and was kept safe all year in the pantry, also a huge cool space and very old fashioned. My favorite confiture was rhubarb. Our cook, Berthe, was the only domestic in our household who was safe from my stepfather's fancy because of her age and talent. She was a darned good cook, who always made sure our supply was plentiful. I remember her standing over those large *cuivre marmite*, her red cheeks shining over the fire. A reminder of her Normand background, with her hands folded over her large belly, proudly admiring her masterpiece.

"Ma P'tite Mam'selle" she would say, "There is no one in whole France who can make confiture like old Berthe can." To which I would heartily agree by sampling most of her goodies—no wonder I was chubby.

My first year in school was very primitive. My walk to school was a good 35 minutes and I had two roads to take. In the spring, accompanied by my maid, we would follow a very rural road lined by old trees and lilacs. Their aroma was entrancing and packs of glycerin fell graciously aside stone walls, adding their own scent to the magic of the place. God, how beautiful nature was back then; how simple its pleasure. How blessed were the children able to enjoy the simplicity of a much kinder, more tender world. In the winter, I preferred taking the *chestnut road*. Trees upon trees of chestnuts lined the trail on my way. By the time I got to school, I almost always had a bellyache from eating too many raw chestnuts.

School consisted of many systems. Teachers back then were the absolute rulers. If you did wrong, you were punished by the teacher, who gave you a note for your father who in turn also punished you with a *fessé*, a spanking on your behind. One of the punishments at school was to stand in front of the class with a donkey's hat on your head, which meant you had acted like an ass.

The most deserving reward was given on Saturday to the best pupil, which was called *La Croix* (the Cross), which was attached to your dress. I only received that honor twice during my three year stay there—which isn't much to say on my behalf.

My teacher would often tell me, "You are one of my most intelligent pupils, but also the most unruly and undisciplined. School for you is one big bore or joke to you." The fact is, she was right. I could never learn from books. Unfortunately, life taught me my biggest lessons the hard way. Mostly daydreaming or counting how many *poux* (lice) the kids in front of me had on them was my biggest past time. My piano teacher, Irene Crouard, turned me against learning to play the piano, which I really loved. For every note I missed, her wooden ruler didn't miss my fingers - God, it hurt! So I refused to learn—a bad mistake I have regretted all my life.

I was a shy child, a loner, but stubborn. I wasn't the most popular, so I kept to myself too much. I was also a very unhappy child—music and books were my world. I must have read every classic I could put my hands on. Very little literary trash was available to kids in those days for which I am deeply grateful. There was and is a great opportunity given to children to read the works of the masters and expand their minds. How I envied their greatness, the righteousness of Gustave Flaubert, the genius of Victor Hugo, and the great knowledge of human heart and wisdom of La Fontaine. They were all there to fancy my imagination and sharpen my mind. They helped me understand and cope with the very hard times ahead and there were to be many! My friends were my books, my escape from loneliness. They had the power to transport me to faraway places, where one always found a way to get out of trouble.

My new life was not a happy one. My stepfather often met with Le Comte de Paris, the next in line to become king. He went alone to these meetings. Our life was very medieval—he was the Master and I felt my mother was there for decoration. Rebellious by nature, I did not fit in and was always in trouble. My happiest time was during vacation with my maternal grandmother; my paternal grandmother had died long ago. Grandma and I always went to Belgium, Ostende, la Panne, and Blankenberg. It was always a joy to go there and being away from him was a special joy in itself.

I loved going to Dieppe in Normandy. They had a medieval

château that always fascinated me. I fantasized about the people who lived there long ago. It must have really been cold and so many stairs to climb. How lonely they must have been and I wondered if there were any ghosts. One particular day, Grandma didn't come, so I went with my mother and stepfather. When I told my mother about my fantasizing about the castle, my stepfather stepped in, "Here she goes again, day dreaming."

I had a weakness as a child, whenever I laughed, I watered my pants—I could not help myself. On that special day, I don't recall what triggered it, except I remember laughing very hard and the inevitable happened. I lost control and wet myself. I tried hiding it, but my embarrassment must have given me away. I remember my mother looking at me shockingly with reproach and saying, "Really, Be'be' you should try to get hold of yourself." I can still see my stepfather's enraged face (although it must have made his day). "I will punish you like the little pig you are!" My mother's weak protest was ignored and she was stopped by his furious glare. She knew better than to insist.

He then proceeded to take us to a newspaper store where he bought a marker and some writing paper on which he wrote in large letters:

"I AM A PIG, I PEE IN MY PANTS"

Satisfied with himself, he made me turn around and

pinned it on both the front and the back of my dress. "Now little pig," he said. "Let's walk."

It must have been a strange procession to the eyes of the onlookers—this trio of two adults followed by a little girl with her head bent down to hide her tears and shame wearing the signs he had written. Since our parade lasted over two hours all over Caen and on the beach, my weakness had been well advertised. Some laughed, while others were sympathetic, and still others pretended not to see it. But they all did and how I hated him!!! From then on, it was his will against mine.

I know my poor mother was suffering. She was not a strong woman—physically, mentally or emotionally. I felt bad for her, but at the same time, resented her weakness. In some strange way, I believe that her weakness made me stronger, so I could deal with people like my stepfather. I always thought that he had a touch of sadistic insanity. After all, his sister died in an insane asylum.

I remember my mother waiting all night for him to come back from one of his so-called *walks.* He was like my father, a womanizer. Poor mother—so little self-confidence and inner strength. The only time I remember her coming to my rescue was when I asked her to nickname me, Line, instead of Jacqueline or Bébé, for which I felt I was getting too old. I can still remember his sadistic chuckle. "Line" (pronounced ligne in French), he said, "Do you know what Line means in English?" I knew some nasty remark would follow and it did. "Well, my dear girl, Line means something that everything and everybody pass on top of." I think that this was probably the first I heard my mother loudly object to his venom. I remember the scene. Only the meaning of his words came to me as I grew older. My mother was not happy, that much I could sense. I tried avoiding confrontation with him for her sake.

We lived in Rouen at that time. My only pleasure was when my grandmother visited us. But to this day, I have yet to understand why my mother told him that her own mother was her aunt. I adored my grandmother and I do believe that she was probably the only person who loved me unconditionally. At 16, she had married the richest man in Angouleme, fifty years her senior—a marriage arranged by her parents. By the time he died, she had six children. She was a very innocent, old-fashioned woman. She then remarried a younger, very charming man who was also a womanizer and managed to give her six more children. He spent all her fortune and left her for another woman. She was still very beautiful at 37. My grandmother's first name was a very old French name, Optat. She never had another man in her life and only lived for her children. She adored me. What

I wouldn't give to have her back, my dear Grandmère.

Life went on and I built a fantasy world, while trying to avoid my stepfather as much as possible. My mother's life was dedicated to pleasing him.

To describe my stepfather, it would be best to picture him in the Middle Ages. He was pale and thin, his hair was cut on *en brosse* (crew cut) and he was very cold. I don't remember him having any kind of humor, except sadistic. No white horse with shining armor was there; only an aristocrat who took his background very seriously. His mother was just as cold and stuck-up.

He put me in the *Pensionnat des Terrasses* School, which was very upscale, run by the *les Soeurs Ursulines*. I was taught what young girls from good families were taught: crochet, Latin, how to walk, never raise your voice, always control your emotions, take yourself very seriously, be in command and how to get ready to learn how to control domestics when you were married. Goodness, I was bored! Although very proper during the day, nights were another matter. I was an *in* student and shared a dormitory with other students. We had our own area, although the areas were separated with drapes.

Although we were very innocent then, some girls would talk about the papa and mama game and giggle, each one putting in her two-cents worth. We would all listen avidly, none of us really knowing what the *expert* was talking about, including the experts themselves. This went on for awhile until we got caught and some of the girls were expelled. Compared to today's morals, it was very innocent and almost laughable, but very unacceptable in our early society. Sex was left unspoken, unacceptable in any conversation. I remember when I was 17, I asked Marie Therese, my girlfriend, "How do people have children?" This was her response, "I think they retire at night and they do something." "What", I asked eagerly. To which she replied, "They kiss, I think."

We had lost our Rouen's home and my "Ursuline's" education. We then moved to Le LaVandou across from my uncle's store in the South of France. It was the home of the town's priest who lived there with a much younger *maid*, whose tasks were very, very questionable.

We occupied the first floor and stayed there a few months. My mother was pregnant and gave birth to a seven-pound daughter, Blanche Anne Marie. Blanche was also the name of my stepfather's mother. A baby girl was much to my stepfather's disappointment. A male child was *de Rigueur* (proper) for an aristocrat. He completely ignored his wife and daughter. My mother's health had deteriorated and his obnoxious behavior added to her suffering. My uncle was sick of my stepfather, so when my sister was two months old, we all returned to Normandy.

Our new home in Elbeuf was bigger than the one in Rouen, but due to bad investments, our lifestyle had been greatly reduced and our domestic staff was down to two.

About the same time as when King George V abdicated his throne to marry Wallace Simpson, the woman he loved, that the fights at my home became more frequent, mostly due to his nightly absences. It was also about this time that my stepfather started sneaking into my room at night and trying to feel my breasts while I was asleep. It would wake me up and I would turn around, pretending I was asleep, trying to avoid him. This happened a few times, until I figured out what to do—I pushed my night table against the door. I never told my mother. She would not have believed me and I was too embarrassed to do so anyway. My mother also had become sicker, so the baby was with us and a maid took care of her.

I went to school, but being shy, I had very few friends. My old friends who lived in Rouen, Josette and Annie, who were Jewish, occasionally came to visit and were very worried about the world news.

The word, War, was often spoken by the adults and it didn't sound very good. Our financial situation had begun to deteriorate, since my stepfather's mother had discontinued her financial contributions. His lack of interest in her business and many disastrous ventures had stopped her help.

My maid, Edith, was a skinny, plain looking girl. We got along just fine and she was not to be pushed around. Our cellar was enormous and like most of them in Normandy, every year it flooded. Edith suggested we take the small boat that was there permanently and go around inspecting all the bottles in their cases. I took the Veuve Cliquot champagne and asked, "Is it good?"

She answered, "I don't know but they sure seem to like it." "Well," I said, "Let's try it." She liked the idea, but was afraid of the consequences.

"I don't know," she said. "My master can be pretty mean." That's all I had to hear, "Let's take one." Opening it was another problem, as when the cork finally popped, so did a third of the champagne. "Veuve Cliquot!"

I recall we kept taking turns sharing the champagne while voyaging in our boat. Well, it didn't take long before the two of us got stoned and sick. We managed to get upstairs just in time to face my mother and stepfather who had arrived from town. Edith and I were holding onto each other, giggling and singing. Of course, they both gasped at the situation, "Where were you?" asked my mother. "In the cellar, of course, can't you see?" barked my stepfather, "And they are drunk!"

This is when I chose to throw up all over his shoes. I

endured another one of his spankings and Edith was fired even though I had taken the blame and told them it was my fault. I guess she wasn't pretty enough and that was a good enough reason for him to fire her.

It wasn't long before our monetary situation had completely deteriorated and forced us to move again, this time into a small apartment also in Elbeuf, where I helped my mother with Blanche after school. I went to Lycée Corneille, a college for both boys and girls. My interest in boys had begun, very innocently, as we all were in that time. I liked the Lycée and made a few friends. Some girls sneaked into the toilet to smoke—it was forbidden, of course, but so cool! I tried it a couple of times, but decided that it wasn't for me. I wasn't a great student and never liked school very much, but I liked this one and felt bad when once again we had to move—this time to an even smaller apartment back in Rouen.

My stepfather tried to get back in his mother's good graces, but he had cost her too much money already. The old lady was very shrewd and money mad, so she didn't fall for his promises of good behavior. We stayed there over a year—one of the worst times amongst many in my life. It was a one-bedroom apartment and I slept in the hallway while Blanche slept in their room.

My mother seemed a little better for awhile. My

stepfather's mother finally resumed some of her financial help. I absolutely detested my stepfather, whom I considered a nasty S.O.B. and avoided being alone with him. Although I was innocent and at a very young age, I sensed he might want to touch me again, as he eventually did and later on, abused his own daughter, too. I was a little fighter, so although I was shy, I was rebellious and able to detect a bad egg—a gift that stayed with me all of my life. Although, I must admit, I did not always follow my instincts.

My maternal grandmother came to stay with us for a while—I loved it when she was there. After she left, our fights amplified. I remember running to a neighbor's apartment with him after me with a strap to beat me up, but the neighbors protected me. Then almost overnight, things changed—my mother took to her bed and never got up again.

War had begun! My stepfather was called into the army— thank God! She cried when he left to go to war. Me, I was ecstatic! How could she love a man who obviously didn't care about her suffering. She had been diagnosed with cancer of the ovaries. After a while, even morphine didn't help. To her last day, she waited for his letters from the battlefield. That was her only happiness. Love is a strange bedfellow.

My Grandma had come back and I overheard my mother tell Grandma, "Please take care of my two daughters." My stepfather's mother also came when the end was near. My mother's crying out in pain followed me all my life. When she died, I refused to stay home and went shopping for a lilac nightgown with money my grandma had given me.

To this day, I don't know why I did it. Criticism was tremendous, especially from my stepfather's mother. I suppose this was my way of helping my pain and celebrating my poor mother's freedom from suffering. My poor grandmother was the only one in deep sorrow. My mother was buried in Rouen in the de Rieux plot. I went back to her grave just once more.

My grandmother and I stayed in the apartment for a couple of months. My Uncle Jean put whatever valuables I had, such as books, jewelry, and paintings into *storage* and I never saw them again.

Bombarding had begun and at the sound of the sirens, we quickly joined the rest of the tenants and made our way down into the cellar. We usually only had to stay there for a couple of hours. Being so young, I found it real *cool*, as did all the young people. At first, the children made it a game until the first bomb fell crashing not far from where we were. Then reality set in and quietness replaced jokes and laughter. This was war!

My grandma seemed to be unusually worried. Sometimes she would look at me and start crying. One day while in the basement, a lady tenant came to talk to us. She knew Grandma and they enjoyed each other's company, talking about their life and crying on each other's shoulders. One specific day, she told Grandma, "We are leaving tomorrow. We can't stay any longer, because the Germans will be here before too long. You should take Jacqueline and go. "Not yet, dear," was my Grandma's reply. "There's still time." "No, No, Optat, there is no time. They will be here very soon, so please listen to me!" Then she put her arms around me and said, "God love you and protect you little one, Shalom." She left the next day and we never heard from her again.

Later on that night, I asked Grandma what the lady had meant. Choking back tears, she took me in her arms, "Child, your father was Jewish. When the Germans come and they will, you will be in great danger."

"What kind of danger," I asked. She ignored my question. "From now on, if someone asks, both your parents were Catholic." "But Grandma that's lying," I objected. "Darling, sometimes in order to survive, we must do things that are not always honorable." How true!

Two days later, bombs started to fall close by. The meaning of fear became real that day. My Uncle Jean, Grandma's son, telegraphed for us to leave immediately. We visited my mother's grave one more time. Then one morning, we were on our way to the South of France.

My paternal family was already in hiding on their beautiful estate in Burgundy where I had visited and played with my cousin many times. My grandma kept her promise to my mother and refused to leave me, so I stayed with her.

The trip was long and difficult since my sister was only a baby. The train was full to capacity with people trying to escape the incoming German Army. Grandma held Blanche on her lap during the 12-hour trip. Being young, I sat on the floor, taking turns to get up and look out the window in awe at the beauty of the scenery. Finally Toulon was called and none too soon. My uncle was waiting for us. My poor grandma was utterly exhausted and my sister extremely cranky and hungry. It took another hour by car to get home to Sanary. Finally we were "home."

It was October 17, 1939. My uncle owned a few optical and photo stores in three towns: Hyeres, Le LaVandou and Sanary. The last town is where we made our home. Tonton Jean rented an apartment for us above a restaurant, La Jeté which was close to his store.

I could see the seaport from my bedroom window. Sanary was a fishing village and very picturesque and lovely with cliffs, beaches and hills where pine trees sprayed their wonderful aroma and scent.

Weeks went by and although the war was raging in the northwest, these were not unhappy times for us in the South.

Unfortunately, food was getting more and more scarce. It was rationed and we were given food tickets mostly for bread. Even with the Black Market always present, the supplies left a great deal to be desired. Grandma would leave early in the morning and walk to different farms in hope of finding food to buy. I would stay home and take care of my sister, Blanche.

My uncle and his wife Suzanne were busy at the store. Grandma did not like Suzanne, because she felt she was too cold and self-centered for her son and whose own family was all that really mattered to her.

The long walks to the farms were taking a toll on Grandma. Her arthritis had become worse and she also suffered with hemorrhoids. There was no pain relief for such things in those days. I felt sorry for my grandma and decided to take her place and go to the farms and stores for food. I must admit that taking care of a baby was not really for me. I can still see her pained expression as she said, "Darling girl, I promised your mother I would take care of you and you are still too young to go by yourself."

"Grandmere," I said firmly, "I am not too young and I made up my mind, so don't worry. I'll be careful." She was crying, "If only your mother was alive." I tried not to show my own hurt.

From then on, I was in charge of supplying the food, with or without ration tickets. I must say I was much better at it than my grandma. I had more nerve and conniving than my sweet grandma would ever have. I was a little of a wheeler-dealer—my Jewish heritage I suppose. Each morning my uncle provided me with a list and I would pedal my bicyclette through town and country in search of milk, bread, rutabaga and whatever I could find. Sometimes I would exchange my ration tickets for fruits and vegetables.

After a rainy night, Grandma would put my sister in a stroller and we would trot to the nearest vegetation and pick up snails that the rains always brought out. We put them in a strainer and covered them with salt for a few days in order to reject water and impurities. Then Grandma would wash them and cover them with garlic, butter and parsley and cook them in the oven ... a specialty in Bourgogne (Burgundy).

But it was not all work. We went to the beach and I made friends with Monique from Paris and Marie Therese, who with her family, had been evacuated from Thionville on the German border, because of the incoming German army. Her father, a well-to-do dentist, resented having to leave all their wealth behind. He was a cold person, a disciplinarian and frustrated for having lost everything. He also resented his daughter's friendliness with me, whom he considered a bad influence. I was too free-spirited and independent. Marie Therese's mother was a typical housewife of that epoque, a real *femme d'intérieur,* whose home and pleasing her husband were her main preoccupations. All of his decisions were final and never questioned by her. She was a fairly nice-looking woman with blue eyes and blonde hair that was starting to turn gray.

Marie Therese was a lovely girl both spiritually as well as physically—5'3", blonde hair, blue eyes and delicate. A complete contrast to my 5'7", brown hair and dark eyes. She was permitted to go out for a walk no more than a couple of hours. We usually walked to the Coline and listened to the crickets. Of course, we talked about boys and our dreams. Her dreams were much less complicated than mine: one love, one husband, one home and children. She was one of the loveliest human beings I ever met in my life—an almost childlike quality about her. She fell in love one day with a friend of mine, Lucien. He was a nice, decent boy whose family were well-to-do farmers and friends of my uncle. They met secretly, but very innocently for about six months. Finally, Marie Therese got the courage to introduce him to her father and mother. Lucien asked her father for her hand in marriage. Ignoring her tears, her father asked him to leave and never see his daughter again. A farmer, even though decent and well-to-do wasn't *good enough* for his daughter. Heartbroken, my dear sweet friend was never the same again. Her already frail health did not improve. Lucien was the great love of her life.

To make things worse, her father forbade her to associate with me, her only friend. In his eyes, I was a menace to his authority and he also blamed me for introducing Lucien to his daughter. "She is a bad influence," he would tell her. I managed, somehow, to see her when he was occupied or away. Marie Therese and I had a signal to let me know—a cloth attached to their tree. She would come out and I would give her news from Lucien and bring him some from her. I would also give her some of the food I had, which was mostly from Lucien. His parents had been warned by Marie Therese's father to keep their son away from her. Eventually, her father got wise and managed to move his family to another town. I truly missed her and worried about her. She had lost her only strength—me. I knew she missed our friendship, which was her only way to get news from Lucien and vice-a-versa.

As it often happens in life, we lost contact. The war was raging and no available communication was possible. It was quite some time after they moved that one of my uncle's friends told us what happened. At the arrangement of her father, Marie Therese married the son of a well-known French General and lost her life giving birth to a baby boy. I sincerely believe she died of a broken heart as did Lucien, who upon learning of her death shot himself and died.

They were both in their twenties—a true Romeo and Juliet tragedy. To this day, at the age of 85, she is still in my prayers and my heart and so is Lucien. My dear, sweet Marie Therese Hirshfell. Life can be so cruel! It has taken me a long time, if ever, to overcome the pain the news of her death brought me.

Many memories during our friendship come back. Like the day we both were at my window looking at the invading German army as they entered our little town of Sanary. We had our first view—on the left was the main road already packed with German equipment, army cars, motorcycles and men in green uniform with casques on their head. They were the picture of strength, organization, invincibility—or so they thought. They were warriors of times gone by and present, an unbelievable scenario that no Hollywood movie could duplicate.

They were an imposing sight, those German. So this was the enemy! How could people of such evil repute be so good looking? After all, wasn't evil supposed to be ugly? They kept on coming. The sound of their artillery was very loud and scary.

Marie Therese spoke German and had a German name, Hirsfell, but her heart was French. She was born in Thionville, which was French or German depending on whoever won the last war.

Marie Therese brought my attention to one soldier in

particular, a giant of a man on a motorcycle, who seemed to be opening the way for the rest of them. He was as big and noisy as life itself; shouting orders to the incoming troops the arrogant conqueror keeping his flock in line terrifying and fascinating to two young innocent girls. Finally, as he was coming back, turning around and shouting orders, he misjudged his decision. During that split second he went full force, head first into a stone wall. "Bon Voyage" I heard my friend say. He was dead, of course. We saw him being carried away, stretched out, as imposing in death as he had been in life.

"Stay away from that window!" Grandma was shouting. "Why, Grandma?" I asked. "Don't ask why, just do as I say!" Her tone was unusually severe. I knew enough not to insist. Grandma had lived through three wars: 1870, 1914 and now 1939. However, young girls will be girls and curiosity was killing us. As soon as Grandma went back to her room to attend to Blanche, muttering something to herself, which sounded like, "Those damn boches (Germans), we tried peeking through the blinds. "Can't see anything," I said exasperated. "Neither can I," echoed Marie Therese. "We really shouldn't," she said reading my mind. I can still remember to this day, such a sweet, pretty girl with beautiful blond hair and big blue eyes. My dearest friend in life, both of us giggling conspiratorially.

"Let's do it," I said, opening the blinds. We sat and rested our arms on the window sill. Now, some infantry troops were standing in front of our building, resting while waiting new orders. Whenever an officer passed by they would extend their hands in the Nazi salute.

Giggling, my friend and I tried imitating them by opening and closing our hands. "Not like that," she said laughing. "Don't you know anything?" She had all of her five fingers extended. Just about then, we became aware that some of the men were looking in our direction, talking and joking among themselves. Then suddenly a pack of them detached from the group and marched towards our building. We could hear the noise of their boots against the pavement and the sound of their casques knocking the steel of the rifles.

Marie Therese and I looked at each other. "I'm scared!" She wasn't laughing anymore and started to cry. Then, after sizing the situation, "Grandma!" I yelled.

We were in the living room now, with Grandma turning white, while we stood there, crying and trying to explain the commotion going on in the stairs. "Oh, my God, children, they are downstairs knocking on their door!" She was thinking fast. "They probably got the wrong apartment, but they'll soon be here. Hurry, hide under the bed!" She was trembling like a leaf. "I'll deal with you later!"

Crawling under the bed wasn't an easy task when you are

in complete terror. Hair, arms, and legs all got in the way. Finally she adjusted the covers around us. "Now, don't you move!" she ordered. We could hear strong knocks from our hiding place. "Who's there," my grandma asked.

"It's me, Mme Dubois." I recognized the voice of our downstairs neighbor. "Oui, oui, je viens, je viens," my grandmother answered. We heard the sound of locks being opened and my grandma's voice trying to sound tough, "What is the meaning of this?"

Then a German voice asking, "Mademoiselle ici?" There are no mademoiselles ici," was my grandmother's answer.

Our neighbor who spoke a little German translated, "These men are looking for a bordello with two girls asking for five francs."

"Yeah, Yeah, Bordello, two mademoiselles," they insisted, forcing their way in. "Bien regardez et partez" (All right, look around and get out). The whole floor shook as they walked into the room where we were. We were told later on that what sounded like a whole army was actually only five soldiers. I could hear my own heartbeat 100 miles a minute. The only mademoiselle they saw was my crying sister, Blanche. They spoke among themselves, looking in every room, and opening doors. Finally, after what seemed like an eternity, they left the room with my grandma on their heels, telling them to get out.

Mme. Dubois told them there were no young girls here and they were mistaken. But of course, she knew better. They entered all the apartments in the building anyway until they were called back to duty, which seemed like forever.

The German terror was gone, but we still had to face Grandma. We came out of our hiding place, expecting the worst. Instead, we found poor Grandma slumped in a chair in sheer exhaustion next to Blanche who had fallen asleep. "I'm sorry, Grandma," I whispered. Marie Therese was behind me, crying in sheer terror.

Grandma didn't answer for a while. When she finally did, tears were rolling down her cheeks. "Please, don't ever take such a risk again, children. This is war. You are innocents and there are a lot of things you don't understand." I could see how hard these words were for her to speak. She cleared her throat, "You see" she went on, "things seem to happen to men during these times." She paused, "It doesn't bring out the best in them. I don't want you to go out alone anymore and your walks to the woods are over. From now on we will pick up Marie Therese and bring her back, unless her parents decide to do it themselves."

She stopped, looking at us as if she was afraid we might object. "One more thing," she added, "we will keep to ourselves what happened today. No need to worry Marie Therese's parents, all right?" Marie Therese ran to her open arms, "Thank you Mme. Delage, thank you so much."

I believe the fear of her father was greater than the one from the Germans. We had learned our lesson. From now on, whatever peeping we did, we did it behind closed blinds. We saw Rommel and Goering pass under my window in their armored cars.

Marie Therese wasn't allowed to come out unless we picked her up and brought her back. It was around this time that she met Lucien through me. I also met Louis whose parents owned the restaurant below -- puppy love, until he took my virginity at 17 ½ without my consent, which today would have been called rape. My other friend was Marguerite whose boy friend was the well known Japanese actor, Sessue Hayakawa, whom she had met in Paris. Another girl I met, Claire, had a crush in Paris on my cousin, Alain, and became our friend. Marguerite and Claire were more worldly than we were and also, five years older.

I remember having a crush on Sessue Hayakawa after seeing the movie "Forfeitures." But then I also had a crush on Nelson Eddy after seeing his movies in the town cinema. Strangely enough, I met him later in life when we both sang in the same club in Buffalo, New York.

The war was getting no better and we anxiously waited for America's intervention, which seemed long in coming. At the same time, we feared the worst as we knew bombarding was inevitable with German troops being here. There was a lot of commotion with the German army. Many were sent here before being shipped to the Russian front and the coming and going was constant.

Food had become very scarce. Whenever I managed to get extra from maneuvering, I would bring some to my Jewish friends who live on the hill—two sisters, Selma and Ruth Blum. They were afraid to leave their home because of the Germans. One day, they were gone without a trace. It was also around that time that my dear friend, Marie Therese moved away - a very hard time. Grandma and my uncle were increasingly scared for me. They felt I wasn't careful enough … taking too many chances.

The disappearance of my Jewish friends, whom people believed had been kidnapped by the Germans in the middle of the night, had been very painful for me. I used to love talking with those ladies. Ruth was badly disabled with a poor heart. Their disappearance, among others, had my grandma and uncle in a state of panic. I wasn't allowed to move as freely as I had before.

I still remember the day the first American bombers flew over our town on a perfect blue-sky afternoon. I was home with Grandma and Blanche, when all of a sudden, a strange sound from far away came to our attention. Very imperceptible at first, then with a steadily increasing roar, like a heavy load that was hard to carry, a sound we eventually recognized as bombers on their way to drop bombs on their designated targets. Bombers coming back from their mission were much faster, with a lighter sound, almost as relief. We came to learn the difference and these sounds have stayed with me the rest of my life.

On that first day, we could only listen and wonder, "What on earth?" My grandma dropped her knitting on the floor as reality set in. As if answering our question, a screeching siren burst forth warning us of approaching bombers. "Oh, my God, we are going to be killed!" Too late to hide, Grandma, Blanche and I just stood there while a wave of bombers passed slowly overhead. We later found out their object was Toulon, a fairly big military town about one hour away from us with a large military fort. Eventually everything became quiet. They had passed over our little town. After a while, muffled explosions from afar were heard.

This was just the beginning of daily terror unless the sky was overcast. The bombers came from 12PM to 2PM depending on the weather. We all used to pray for rain and although we had never been hit, we knew that it was only a matter of time. The Germans were here and had built a few blockades, one next to our building.

One early afternoon, as Grandma, Blanche and I came back from visiting my uncle, that too familiar sound began like the purring of an enormous cat, the noise increasing as it came closer. Only this time, the sound seemed different. The siren had started. I don't know what made me do it, but I screamed, "Let's go!" I grabbed Blanche and pushed Grandma from the kitchen toward the door, not yet understanding what was happening. "Let's go!" I repeated. I grabbed her hand and, at first, she resisted. Finally, she allowed herself to be pushed toward the stairs and almost fell. "Are you crazy, child?" she cried. I ignored her and instead I screamed, "Please hurry the planes are coming here!" The alarm in my voice and the sirens must have convinced her, for my poor old grandma never moved so fast. As we reached the street, two German soldiers with their helmets on came running past us.

Still dragging Grandma and holding Blanche, I pushed through the door of the restaurant with my foot. Some people were already standing inside. A new strange noise could be heard like a train entering a station. It was a bomb that fell and then exploded. The noise was deafening! As it exploded, the deflagration sent some of us flying into the next room along with chairs, tables and everything in its path. The whole thing lasted a few minutes, followed by a deathly silence, then cries of the wounded. I could barely hear my grandma screaming my name and Blanche's. The explosion from the bomb triggered a wall of dust, which made us unable to see anything past our feet.

Half-deaf, in shock and bleeding, with Blanche crying next to me, but OK, I wanted my grandma. "Grandma, Grandma!" I yelled. "Baby, where are you?" "We are here, Grandma, its OK." It was impossible to see anything. People around us were crying with pain. As the dust was slowly settling, our amazement soared at the amount of destruction around us. As I strained my eyes, I made out my grandmother standing, trying to locate us. "Over here, Grandma, over here!" I yelled. She made her way toward us, avoiding the debris. She was covered with dust and her hair was standing on end from the deflagration. Blanche's hair and mine were the same—it took us a week to get it combed out. Grandma looked like a ghost, but alive. We didn't look much better, but I must say that Blanche reacted very well. I couldn't believe that we were still alive!

The sirens finally gave the end of the alert. Wounded people lay waiting for whatever help they could get. My wound to my leg wasn't great and I was able to walk. Blanche was just fine, as I had fallen on top of her and my body became her shield. Leaning on Grandma, we walked toward the same door we had entered—only the door was gone.

The German soldiers we had passed on our way into the restaurant were dead—a bloody mess. The bombs had done their destructive work. Some buildings had been hit directly.

The street was unrecognizable with all sorts of debris and in complete disarray. The Germans were running back and forth. The blockade next to our apartment building was mostly destroyed. Broken boats were nonchalantly floating on the water. Only the sky remained a blasé blue, unaffected by men's folly—kind of a dejá vu sort of thing from other centuries of madness, the original curse of the human race, greed and power.

Grandma was very quiet, probably thanking God for our lives. People were slowly starting to come out of their hiding places. Going back to our apartment was unthinkable. The building had been badly damaged. However, my uncle and his wife were all right and so was their store.

That day was only the beginning of steady bombing. We managed to salvage some of our belongings and bring them to a small house located on the outskirts of town that my uncle rented for us. It was a lovely little house facing a field of wheat. I slept in the living room and Grandma and Blanche in the bedroom. In spite of everything, strangely enough it was a time I will remember with great love and melancholy. Halas! My stepfather was sent back from the army because of a wound. He came back to claim his daughter, Blanche. Grandma was heartbroken. It was very hard saying goodbye to my sister, whom I only saw once more, thirty years later — and that was her own decision which was heartbreaking. From now on it was Grandma and me. Seeing my stepfather again had re-opened my total dislike for the man. I was glad to see him go, even if it sadly meant taking my sister with him.

Halas! I was getting hard to control. I would leave against my grandma's wishes and come back with perfumes I had taken from a store called, Le Grand Tule, owned by my aunt's sister-in-law. When she was busy attending customers, I helped myself to perfume and silk. Grandmother found out and didn't know what to do. If she brought everything back, it would surely get me in trouble, but keeping it would eventually do the same.

I had a valise full of the goods when I told Grandma—the poor dear turned white. She came up with the idea of hiding the suitcase at our neighbor's house under the pretext of hiding it from my uncle. "You see," she told them, "he doesn't know that my granddaughter is collecting German paraphernalia. If you could keep it for just a little while." They heartily agreed and told us to leave the case that night at their door and they would take care of it.

Well, as it turned out, the suitcase and its contents were *stolen by some unknown person,* or so they said. Looking back and so much wiser, I have to laugh for bringing my case to people who had seen us coming: a nervous old woman and an inexperienced young girl with guilt written all over our faces.

As I grew older, I became even harder to control. I was a pretty girl and the French and German men and later on the Italians were after me. Of course, I loved the attention. I remember one very handsome German officer who kept following me whenever our paths would cross in town. Well, I'm sure I'm not the first maiden in all these centuries whose heart melted at the sight of a handsome enemy soldier.

One evening there was a knock on the door. My grandma was asleep in her room, so I answered. There he was with his bodyguard standing away from him. He asked me in his educated French if he could see me. Well, it's amazing how fast you forget the rules of decency when you are young and hot-blooded. A war! What war? Ironically, I found that flirting with a German officer was very funny and excitingly dangerous. Funny because he didn't know I was Jewish and dangerous for the same reason. I don't try to apologize nor will I. The quality or lack of it in a man is not in the uniform he wears, but in himself.

He signaled his man to wait outside while I let him in. We spoke for a long time. He was very sad and missed his family. He found my address by having his man follow me. He resented being part of the war and the brutality of it. He hated the Gestapo, whom he called the murderous clowns of Germany. He was a decent quiet man caught, as many were, in the midst of insanity. I never mentioned my Jewish background and he felt good having found a sympathetic female to talk to. We kissed and became lovers and when he left three hours later, we knew we could never meet again for security reasons. We agreed not to look at each other when passing in the street. His regiment left a week later. In my heart, I wished him well. I never told my grandma. For me it had been the thrill of danger pushed to the limit. I often wonder if he would have sold me out if he had known. To this day, I don't believe so.

Many times before, my uncle had to hide me from the SS who asked my uncle if I was a Jew. His answer was always an outraged, "Of course not!" Even a colonel of a battalion at the time wanted me for his *girlfriend*. My uncle told him I had left with a guy, he didn't know where, when in reality he was hiding me in his house.

My first boyfriend, Louis Leydet the son of the owner of the restaurant in our first apartment, had left for the army with promises of eternal love. One day my friend, Claire, came to say goodbye. Her family had rented a home in the country about ½ hour by bicycle from where we were. "You and your family should leave, Jacqueline," she said. "It is not safe here with all the planes bombing."

We made plans to visit each other every other week. She left the next day with her parents, two cousins and a brother. She was a very pretty, perky fun girl.

Two days later, we had the worst bombing of all. Strangely enough, it was not in town, but outside. They were trying to hit a German artillerie. We were told later that one bomb was a direct hit on Claire's house. They were all killed. God love her! Only my friend, Monique, was left, but very taken with Sessue Hayakawa.

From now on, things became much worse for the Germans. Hitler was pulling most of his troops from the south of France only to send them to his Waterloo, the Russian front. God, you'd think he had learned from Napoleon and would stay away from that awful cold and snow.

Now the flamboyant Italians were occupying our town. They sure were more fun than the Germans. "Schöen," was replaced by, "Que Bella Bambina." I can still see them. I could swear each one must have been carrying a mandolin instead of a gun! Unlike their forefathers, Roman ancestors, warriors they were not. One day looking out the window of my uncle's apartment, I remember one imposing officer sitting tall on his horse, with a feathered hat. What a majestic figure he was! Of course, he had seen me and ordered his subordinate to serenade me with his mandolin, J'attendrai (French for 'I Will Wait'). It was very impressively romantic, but not to Grandma who must have been in a bad mood for before I could stop her, she sent a *pot de chambre* (chamber pot) flying out of the window right on top of the two serenading troubadours. Poor Grandma! She had to fight so many times for my *honor* that she simply had run 'out of tools. However, that didn't discourage lover boy, whose name I later learned was Prince Mario Mantaboli.

Between the bombings and lack of food, life was very difficult. Troops came and went—there were 100 men for every woman. But hands off! No one was to fraternize with the enemy. Those who did paid the price. I was the lucky one.

Then came the day my uncle, his wife, Suzanne and Grandma moved from Sanary to LeLavandou. I was left behind to care for his store. After all, I was 18 and most of the troops in Sanary had been called elsewhere. As I recall my days as an optician at the tender age of 18, I cannot help but chuckle. Good God! I was at my Jewish best then. I could have sold a pair of prescription lenses to anyone with 20/20 vision. Not bad for someone whose only training came from my uncle. I can still see myself very professionally placing those click-on lenses in place on people's noses until the strength suited their eyes. Back then, strength went by numbers. I would then put the right ones into their selected frame. If the frame was too light, I would pass them over the flame to enlarge them - many cracked, leaving a void in the inventory. Also, some people came back to tell me that their new eyeglasses made them cross-eyed. Calling my uncle was impossible, because some of the money I received from these glasses, I had kept. However, the rest I kept for my uncle to calculate on his weekly visit. He figured it out, because people complained and within six months, he closed his Sanary store and took me with him to LeVandou. The last time I had been there was with my Mother, stepfather and new sister.

German troops were still there. My uncle was the only optician, underwater equipment retailer and photograph developer around. I learned how to develop the pictures, but did not stay very long at it, because of the porno pictures taken by the German soldiers. My uncle then put me up front in sales.

My grandma was happy to have me back and we both shared a little house near the beach. These were fairly good times, but my grandma lived in terror of my fooling around. I was a pretty girl and men were in great supply. In those days, it didn't take much to be labeled 'loose.' I was very stubborn and I suppose I gave them a hard time. I could not wear lipstick then—my uncle told me only loose women did.

A tall good-looking German by the name of Eric Sellman used to come to the store for pictures. He was quite taken with me. My uncle was very aware of it. "Those damn *chleux* (German)," he would mumble under his breath. What I thought he didn't know is that I met him in 'private' on a deserted side of the beach. But nothing was private in those days, so it was told to my Uncle who had a terrible fit! It really looked bad for him, since he was now the Honorary Mayor of the town. He then forbade me to go anywhere except to the stores.

One afternoon as I was crossing the street to go to the produce store next to the railroad station, the sound of sirens began to send their warnings. As I stood there wondering what to do next, the too familiar sound of planes slowly approaching sent an icy cold feeling up and down my spine. Civilians and soldiers alike were running in search of shelter. Then the 'train whistle' could be heard. I stood there like an idiot waiting to be killed.

All of a sudden I felt myself being pushed to the ground with someone on top of me. Just then, a bomb hit and exploded. This bombarding only lasted a few seconds. We found out their target was Toulon. The person on top of me disembarked slowly and spoke, "Are you all right?" As I tried getting up, that someone's bleeding hand took mine to help me.

"Thank you," I managed to say. Standing up, I looked at my benefactor—it was Eric Sellman. A German had tried to save my life … how ironic. He was bleeding from his leg and arms. Again, the same question crossed my mind—had he known my Jewish ancestry, would he have done it?

I was becoming badly paranoid, but with good reason.

Around us were wounded and two dead. A friend of mine, Alice, was screaming and shaking violently. When I reached her, I realized she was only having a nervous attack. I left to let someone else take care of her and went home.

My grandma and uncle were in complete panic. I'll never forget her face when she finally saw me, her beloved granddaughter. "Oh! Thank God!" she whispered and cried even more. When I tried to tell my uncle what happened, he brushed it aside. The house hadn't sustained much damage, aside from some plaster and neither did my uncle's store, his upstairs apartment or own house. Lucky, I guess. From then on, I stayed at home or at the store.

The battle was raging in Normandy. As I was attending a client one day, five Gestapo SS soldiers came in. I especially remember one, who was short and skinny—a nervous little man walking back and forth and staring at me, but not in a flirty way. He gave me the creeps, so I tried avoiding his fixed gaze and made myself busy, but my uncle caught on. This was trouble and I could smell it. In his black uniform, he looked like a nasty cockroach all dressed up. Finally, he approached me. "What's your name?" he snapped trying intimidation. Using the same technique, "Jacqueline," I answered looking him straight in the eyes. His cold blue eyes didn't flicker. "Last name?"

"Delage," that was my Uncle's name. He seemed to be

trying to make a decision when my uncle intervened. "Here is a wonderful camera you might be interested in." That's what they had asked for when they came in. Some of them also bought film to take pictures and others sunglasses.

One of the SS who was watching their armored car came in excitedly and spoke to them. They must have received some important orders, because they all left in a hurry, but not before the skinny one turned around and said, "We'll be back." Never was I so happy to see someone go! That did it! No more store for me! My uncle told me that they were trained to recognize Jews by looking at them. They did come back a week later asking for me. My uncle told them that I went to Paris to get married. Nevertheless, they asked the question, "Is she a Jew?" to which my uncle, trying to be an actor, exploded in laughter and said, "Of course not, we are all Catholics here." The fact is, I was hidden above the store. Now I was even afraid to go out at all. Where are the Americans? We were all waiting!

We knew the bombing was part of the campaign to clean out the German forces. We had all heard about the American ships that were coming to the shore of Normandy. It must have been an unexpected, unbelievable sight for the German army to visualize the sea covered with the mighty American ships on May 6, 1945. Now we waited for our turn.

That evening my grandma had prepared dinner. Lately my

uncle had decided that we all must sleep in the apartment above his store, in case of an emergency. By 9 PM, we were all in bed - Uncle Jean, Suzanne, Grandma and me. Before I fell asleep, I was kidding Grandma, telling her that when she was asleep I would cut her hair. That made her mad, because she loved her long hair, which she wore in a *chignon* (bun). Being young, I was insensitive, but that goes with the territory.

We must have been asleep for quite some time when the phone rang. Apparently it had rung for a long time, because it woke Grandma and me. I heard my uncle answer. His voice became agitated, so sensing trouble was coming, Grandmother got up and left the room. I could hear what sounded like gunfire from faraway. All of a sudden, my uncle and Grandma flew into the room. "Get up! The disembarkation has started." Later I learned that Eric Sellman had called to warn us to leave. When you are young, danger is far away from the mind—only the excitement remains. Oh boy! I thought finally some action! Oh boy, indeed—little did I know.

After quickly assembling our valuables, clothes, some food and water, we left in a hurry. My Aunt Suzanne was constantly crying and whining out of fear. My uncle directed us to the cemetery, our designated hideaway. It took us about 20 minutes on foot to get there … not far, really. My Uncle had phoned some friends to join us. They met us halfway there—Martin, Julie, their 11-year-old daughter, Denise, and a dog, which made my uncle very upset. "Why did you bring a dog?" he snapped. "Don't you know it—he could have us killed if he barks?" "I want my dog," Denise cried. They promised to keep him quiet.

It was 3 AM when we arrived. The cemetery was not big. We followed my uncle to the back of the cemetery and came to a narrow impasse, a 25 feet long, but not wide enough to stretch our legs. A stone wall was hiding the graves, which were facing us. At out backs, a forest stood on higher ground hiding us. We all took a seat in the impasse. Access to a trail going in or out of the forest was over to our left. On our right where we came in was a dead end. I placed my backpack to the left of me. Grandma sat on my right and next to her were my uncle and aunt. Gunfire was getting louder, although it was still far away.

Around 4:30 AM, we heard people walking around the cemetery. My uncle signaled us to hush. Then someone called out softly, "Jean, are you here?" What a relief for my uncle who answered, "Over here, Pascal, over here." It was my uncle's friend, Pascal Larmont, his wife, Jane, and her brother, Jacques. "Don't use the light," my uncle warned. By then, enough daylight could direct them slowly to our hideaway. They all settled down to my left.

"You know, Jean," spoke Pascal, "the Americans have

arrived in St. Claire. That's 100km away." "Great!" my uncle answered. The danger was on everyone's mind. Around 5:30 AM, two more and the last of my uncle's friends, Philipe and Marc, joined us. By then our little hideaway was full to capacity with 12 of us. Philipe sat next to my backpack and Marc next to Susan.

The dog had kept fairly quiet except for a few barks at the sight of wild animals passing by. By then, night was nearly over. Our human needs were the most embarrassing, especially for us women. So we decided men would go on the right and women to the left where the trees afforded more privacy.

Having settled that problem, water was the biggest issue of all. The number of days we were going to have to stay there were anyone's guess. By 7 AM, the sun was already hot and with daylight came a new fear, being discovered by the Germans.

Philipe kept making jokes to keep our minds off the inevitable. He was a tall, skinny man in his thirties who had been rejected by the army because of a bowel disorder! Marc was about the same age and was disqualified for service because one leg was shorter, while Pascal suffered from an asthmatic condition. All three were heartbroken for not having been able to serve. My uncle, in his fifties, had been gassed in the first war of 1914 and his lungs were badly affected. Pascal had brought a gun with him, which all the men agreed should only be used in case of extreme necessity.

Up to this point, Denise thought the whole situation was exciting, but not me, since I already had a taste of war. My aunt was constantly complaining about the lack of facilities and comfort. At one point, my uncle finally told her to shut up!

The first day in our hideaway was spent without incident. However, the fighting was getting closer. Our water rations had been minimized, so the heat made it hard to bear. On our second day, we had all settled in and ready to sleep when suddenly, we heard someone coming from the forest walking slowly toward our impasse on the left. The knocking of a rifle against probably his canteen told us the story. Without a sound, we all came to life. He seemed to be alone. The dog! There was nothing any one of us could do. Thank God, the sky was pitch black. As he slowly passed, the sound of the rifle hitting his canteen became louder and shakier. I swear he was as scared as we were. Then he disappeared. Why was he alone? He could have machine-gunned us all. Was he deserting? He never did stop or turn our way—he was just a strange lonely figure in a crazy world. The dog never barked!!!! It was really and truly a miracle, one of those strange happenings in life with no logical answer.

We were becoming tired, feeling dirty and more nervous than before. The heat of the sun didn't help. Grandma's arthritis and hemorrhoids were pretty bad, but even my young body was hurting and Denise was becoming very difficult. The fighting sounded very close. It was our fifth day there, so our water supply was almost gone and so was the food, except for some nuts.

By midmorning, my uncle told everyone to "Shush" and his finger pointed toward the sky. There were planes coming in our direction, flying fairly low. "Who are they?" someone asked. "R.A.F.," my uncle replied, lowering his binoculars. "Oh! Merde (shit)!" We knew, that unlike the American bombers, the R.A.F. were known to strike with deadly accuracy, practically on top of their targets.

Probably mistaking us for Germans, they started firing and all hell broke loose. "Everyone get down!" my uncle screamed. Grandma had thrown me to the ground, her arms around me. Bullets from the machine guns were flying all around us and for the first time in my young life, I found out what fear really was. Someone was crying in pain. I could hear Denise screaming. The noise was deafening. Then, they were gone. But the nightmare had just begun.

The awakening was brutal—next to me, my bag was transversed with bullets. Philippe was dead, while Denise held her head in her hands and was making strange sounds. I was trembling and couldn't stop. Someone's blood was on my arms. Pascal was holding his arms, which were covered with blood. Jane, his wife, was trying to help him. The planes were gone, but our misery had just begun. Poor Philippe had been hit on the head. The men were deliberating on what to do with his body. However, the most pressing priority was to take care of the wounded, because we had very little medication and certainly not the kind we needed.

The heat that day was extreme, which made it worse for Pascal who also was having an asthmatic attack. The men had taken Philippe's body across the impasse where the woods began and covered it with branches and leaves. Truly heartbreaking! Some of the remaining water had to be used to clean up the wounds. Thirst is much worse than hunger, but leaving our hideaway would have been suicidal. The dog had been killed and Denise wouldn't let anyone take it away.

The rest of the day was spent in fear, sweat and thirst. Marc grieving the loss of his friend, Philippe, spent most of the day rocking his body back and forth, tears running down his face. Pascal was in pain and so was Julie, who had been hit in the shoulder. Jacques and Jane were OK, as were my uncle, Grandma and Susan. Again a miracle. None of my family had been hit. My uncle was finally able to talk to Denise and take her dog away to be buried.

The fighting was very close now. We spent one more night where none of us slept. Around 4 AM, the fighting was taking place in LaVandou, so we could hear it, but it didn't last long.

Finally, the American and French troops arrived. We heard shouting very close, "It's over, It's over!" My uncle decided to wait until 9 AM to move us back to town, while the wounded had to wait for a carriage and help.

Martin, who was OK, decided to wait with his wife, Julie, but asked us to care for Denise and take her with us. We left at the designated time to walk to town or 'Dante's Inferno.' Marc was holding Denise in an effort to stop her from seeing the carnage. Good God! Soldiers were lying dead or wounded—some with part of their body missing. We had to step over them to reach our destination. I threw up. Marc was holding Denise's eyes closed. Shaking badly, I held on to Grandma's arm. I tried closing my eyes, but just couldn't. The horror held its fascination.

American and French soldiers were everywhere. We finally reached our home, but the windows had been blown away. However, the Grand Hotel was livable, so my uncle got two rooms there.

The same day we arrived, I had a nervous breakdown, screaming and carrying on—I was a mess. Without the love of Grandma, I don't know what I would have done.

I finally calmed down and went into the village with my uncle, shaking hands with our saviors! What a handsome bunch they were. They were unlike the German's frigid personality who took everything seriously or the Italians who were the opposite and thought that music could fix anything, but so charming. In contrast, the American's easy going, lucky attitude, made them sexy and lovable. Lots of fun, but when serious matters had to be done, they were there—all men. They had a childlike quality in them, but were so attractive, easy to be with, and possessed a sense of humor lacking in the Germans. My uncle, being the Honorary Mayor, shook hands with most of them. What a joy! On our way back to the hotel, we saw Germans attached to trees, being held prisoners. Some of my uncle's customers were wounded. One had wounds in his throat pretty bad and couldn't talk, but his eyes told his suffering. I remember him, because he was the one who kept showing the picture of his children to my uncle.

Only American and French wounded soldiers were taken to the Red Cross, in priority. Fair! However, fair isn't a word that belongs in any war.

Some civilians were killed right there on the spot where they were held if they had collaborated with the enemy. Others trying to get away were gunned down. Also attached to a tree was Eric Sellman, the enemy who tried saving our lives. The heart of a man is not to be judged by the uniform he was made to wear.

The next morning a commotion from the street below

woke us. Opening the window and looking down, we saw a mob of people surrounding some young girls who were standing on a platform shaking and looking scared. "What is this all about?" I asked Grandma. My uncle had just come in and answered for her. "They had German boyfriends."

Suddenly a man I didn't recognize jumped on the stand brandishing a pair of large scissors, shouting, "It's payback time f- - -whore, for sleeping with the enemy!" Then grabbing one of the girls, he proceeded shaping her beautiful red hair. I will always remember her face as she spoke, "Do what you want, I don't care. He is dead and so am I—he was my life!" The last of her lovely hair fell to the floor. I don't know why I started crying. She stood there looking so vulnerable. The price of love—somehow women always pay the price.

The next girl became hysterical and another man came up to restrain her while her hair was being cut. This is when I lost it and my screams became intertwined with hers. It was my second breakdown. I was kept under sedation for the next two days. I found out later on that my uncle used his power to keep me from succumbing to the same fate.

Meanwhile the fighting kept going on in the next towns over. When I felt well enough, I went with my Uncle to a bistro where he had invited a bunch of French and American soldiers for a welcoming drink. When we arrived, right across from the bistro, lined against a wall were three German soldiers awaiting sentencing. My uncle told me, "The one in black is an SOB of a *Boche* (German). He is responsible for many tortures and deaths." The German's eyes met mine and in them I saw extreme fear and pleading—I quickly turned mine away. This was a man who wouldn't have hesitated to send me to Warsaw had he known I was a Jew.

Since the debarkation, many things were discovered, like a list of people to be shipped away to Germany. My name was among them. Someone must have found out about my father.

People were spitting and mocking the three Germans. Every tree in town had a German attached to it. Although thrilled that this hell was over, I could not bring myself to humiliate the fallen—no matter how evil. Their punishment will eventually come from a Higher Judge.

Troops were constantly moving. I made friends with some of them and, as destiny would have it, I also met my future husband, as well as one of the great loves of my life. My uncle had invited a few GIs and French soldiers for a meal and wine. We had moved back to our original home near the beach. They all were fine young men, very outgoing and, of course, like any young girls, I was instantly captivated and being pretty didn't hurt my cause either. I had more than my choices of beaus. Amongst them, I met Albert whom I eventually married, Thornton whom I would love and Louis who became my dearest friend. We all made friends and exchanged names and addresses. I found out that Albert was an English and French teacher in Boston College and 20 years older than I. He was nice looking, 5'7" and could have been the twin of George Raft in looks. He was a nice man, probably too nice for my undisciplined, rebellious ways. His battalion moved on shortly after we met.

Louis Guadagnoli came from Algeria of French parents. His twin brother had recently been killed in the war and Louis had a premonition that he would be next. He was a tall, handsome, decent young man who loved his family. He had been wounded and was sent to a northeast battle where eventually, he did lose his life, my dear, dear friend who had given me so much good advice. His broken hearted parents kept in contact with me for a long time. They had lost two sons. He did love me, but my feeling for him had been strictly platonic.

Only Thornton's battalion stayed in Hyeres, the next town over. Thornton was from Turlock, California and married. Although other young men were interested, including the son of a famous stockings maker and another, whose family owned a great farm in New York state. Thornton was the only one …

Many wounded soldiers kept coming to the town's hospital, which used to be a casino. I told my grandma that I wanted to enroll as a volunteer. After their initial objections, both my grandma and my uncle agreed. Exactly two doctors and two nurses, plus volunteers like me took turns in different shifts.

The hospital consisted of Room A, a huge room crowded with beds and occupied by wounded soldiers. Room B was much smaller, but only treated soldiers who had been burned. Most of them had been trapped inside their burning tanks. The smell from that room was nauseating.

Room C we called 'oubliettes' (oblivion), where soldiers beyond help were left. I recognized one as the German SS in black who had been lined against the wall, whose eyes had crossed mine. I learned later the F.F.I. (Force Française de l'Intérieur) had purposely removed their handcuffs one night, allowing them to go. It became a cat-and-mouse game as the men fled with the FFI at their heels. Two were killed on the beach and the third one (in black) had a bullet lodged in his throat. Next to him was a Frenchman, who had been hit in the bowels and could not be operated on.

Upstairs was another matter—Senegalais (corps of French Army colonial infantry from Senegal, French West Africa) occupied the whole second floor. This was to be one of my chores—making sure that everything was OK there. I never made it to the second floor that morning. My duties started the next day and with them the shock of my life …

I started promptly at 3 PM and as I came in, so did

many wounded soldiers. I was called in to help the nurse. My assignment then was to undress the soldier and report the wound to the nurses. They were such young men. As a novice, I nearly fainted when upon trying to remove a soldier's boot, his foot came off with it! A nurse, already used to this, promptly stuck smelling salts under my nose. I felt so embarrassed after this that I tried controlling my emotions from then on.

By 4 PM that same day, I started in Room A. A routine checkup, really mostly a recuperating room where medication was given to the patients whenever available. Morphine was in small supply and only badly wounded soldiers were given some. I found out that talking to them was almost as important as drugs—a smile and a word of encouragement went a long way.

Room B was more difficult. It was the burn unit and the smell was very bad. Strangely enough, third-degree victims were almost without pain, mostly shaking in shock.

I remember one man in particular, whose name was Marc. He was so badly burned, his skin was completely off so you could see his bones, yet he was joking with me, asking for wine and a date. When I left the room, I threw up. To this day, I can remember the smell—indescribable. Marc died that same night.

Room C must have been a copy of what hell must be like.

The Germans had no medication and were in deep pain and begging for a doctor. I would nod my head, yes, knowing it to be a lie. A Frenchman laid there whose stomach wounds were so bad it was impossible to operate on them.

His stomach had ballooned to the extreme. He kept calling the name of a woman, Jeanne. I sat next to him holding his burning hand. Opening his eyes, he asked, "When will they operate?" Once again, I lied as I said, "Soon, very soon." He relaxed a little, passed gas and apologized. "It helps," he said. "It's okay," I told him, "It's okay." He started crying, "I want to go home."

"You will," I lied again. His eyes followed me as I left. "I'll be back," I promised. I went outside and wept.

I then went directly to the doctor and told him about the men in Room C. "They are beyond help." His tone was final. "But they do need morphine, Doctor," I said. He was a tall, strict no-nonsense man, sweating and near exhaustion. "Understand this, young girl. Our priority is in the operating room!" Having said that, he walked away. I was left standing there, not knowing what to do.

Just then, Nurse Irene walked by, her uniform covered with blood.

"Rough day?" she asked. "Yes," I mumbled. She was a tall lanky blond with kind green eyes. She nodded her head. "We lost three boys today. It stinks - I hate this F - - - - - war!"

She wiped her hands on her uniform and looked at me. "You need something?" "I just asked Dr. Martin for morphine for Room C. She opened her eyes wide, "You're kidding!" I didn't reply. "No, I guess you're not. Don't do that again." I was going to ask why not, since he is a doctor and morphine might become available.

Abruptly, she changed the subject and told me, "Now is the time for you to go and get acquainted with the second floor. She looked at me over her eyeglasses, "You'll have to see if everything is OK and write down the complaints." Saying that, she handed me a notebook and pen, "As of now, you're on your own, except for reports." Then she walked off after handing me a key.

I don't know why, but my stomach felt very queasy all of the sudden. I had heard about the second floor and its reputation. The last nurse's aide had left screaming and running down the stairs—never to come back.

Taking the advice of Nurse Irene, I braced myself and climbed the still beautiful stairway made for a different world. Facing the top of the stairs was a large imposing door with a gold handle. Even though I had braced myself, nothing prepared me for what was inside. The door squeaked as I opened it with the key. The room was dark and as my eyes became adjusted, suddenly there they were! Men! Black men, seated on the floor, each with their red Fez tassel dangling on the side of their head, all staring at me. Fear had my feet glued to the floor unable to run away. The stench was nauseating. Some were obviously wounded with stained bandages. Yet, very little noise came from the room.

Unknown to me, Nurse Irene had followed me up the stairs. She touched my arm and I jumped. "These are Senegalais," she said. She was an American nurse who spoke French—a tough cookie, top notch, no-nonsense nurse who loved her job. I admired her and we became friends.

"What kind of necklaces are these?" I whispered, pointing my finger. "Their trophies," she sounded amused. Encouraged by my silence, she continued. "These are German's ears that they cut off once they became their prisoners and made necklaces out of them—the more ears, the more important they become." Once again, I found myself on the floor with smelling salts to my nose. After that day, I really tried keeping my emotions in check. Although benevolent, I was proud of my job. I did not mention my second floor chores to my uncle or my Grandmother, who would surely have forbade me to go.

No firearms were allowed on the second floor. However, they were allowed their knives, which they always kept and sorry would be those who tried taking them away. Many of the men had marks on their faces, a distinction of their tribes. Amazingly, the second floor turned out to be a rewarding experience, after my fear and repulsion of their strange ritual diminished. They were like big children who laughed a lot and very appreciative of whatever help you gave them. They were so proud of their bravery in combat. Their loyalty to their motherland was legendary. I came to understand and respect their way of life. In the days that followed, I tried supplying them with medication and cleaning up their wounds. They were extremely respectful, never complaining. Their big smiles greeted me each day. They called me, "Mimizelle," their way of pronouncing Mademoiselle. Their French was atrocious, but understandable. They were so proud of their trophies. Their 'necklaces' were their pride and joy. Not wanting to offend them, I told them it was against my religion when they asked me to try on one of them. One day when I came in, they were getting ready to go back to the front. The wounded were sent to Toulon. Caring for them was one of my most memorable and touching memories of the war. I only stayed there three weeks. The wounded in Room B had died, along with so many others. The hospital moved on to Toulon to be closer to the battles.

I then became Thornton's "girlfriend." He couldn't speak French, nor I English—love has its own language. I tried bringing him to my family one evening, but they refused— so embarrassing! I decided then to leave home, so I enlisted in the French Army.

The Battailon des Maures caserne (military barracks) were located in Hyeres, about 40 minutes from home. I simply walked in one day and went directly to the French Colonel's office. He was a tall, distinguished gentleman whom I told with my usual nerve that I would make a wonderful secretary. My references were the very best. He looked at me, not quite knowing what to make of me and asked, "Can you type?" I wasn't about to say no. "Oh, absolutely," I replied. "What the hell," I thought, "after all it doesn't take a genius to do that."

He thought it over. "Very well," he replied. "I need a secretary anyway, but young lady, you will work for me and the Doctor, as well as inspect the prisoners and report their needs to me and the Doctor." That is how I became Secretary Chiffreuse to the Battalion des Maures, the only woman among 5,000 men, French soldiers and German and Italian prisoners. I became an Honorary Lieutenant shortly after that.

I enjoyed every minute of it, but never flirted with any of the men. I took my job very seriously. They dressed me in the most unflattering heavy army uniform with an enormous wide belt and army boots. None of the fancy dresses I later wore in life could compare with the pride I felt wearing that ugly outfit.

Some of the officers resenting my presence at the lunch table, letting me know it by using bad manners, like taking out their false teeth, telling dirty jokes and passing gas. I didn't care, because I was where I wanted to be. The inspection of the prisoners was something else. Unlike the Senegalais who spoke French, these were German and Italian prisoners. I almost had to use sign language. There was a German man suffering from a bad tooth, so he showed me with his fingers; others did the same. I found one man among the Italians who could understand some of the three languages, so I took him with me on my rounds. Being the only woman among almost five thousand men was strange and very unusual.

The Colonel and I became friends and he took me under his wing. He was very much in love with his wife and I with Thornton, so no problem there … strictly friendship. Being a Secretaire Chiffreuse involved receiving and sending secret information, which I did very well. However, once the Colonel realized that my typing and shorthand left a lot to be desired, he assigned me to more responsibilities and less bureaucracy.

Dr. Legrand requested my help twice a week. Every so often, the dear doctor would tell the men to lower their pants and underwear, so he could check their private parts. Those who didn't pass the inspection would get a shot in their derriere. On my first day there, I didn't know where to look. Keeping a straight face was not easy while staring at their bare asses. Some men were laughing, while others were as embarrassed as I was. Those needles at that time were heavy and painful. One day, one man farted as he got stuck with the needle. I buried my head into my desk trying to control my laughter. Dr. Legrand's severe stare brought me back to order. It didn't take me long to get used to the scenario and behave accordingly. Soon thereafter, I was given a new responsibility.

Twice a week the officers used to meet at a home not too far from the barracks. They played cards and liked to hear music. We had a German prisoner who was an excellent pianist. My duty was to bring him to and from that home to play from 7 to 9 PM. I asked for a soldier to accompany me even though I was carrying a 45. That place wasn't safe, because a few Germans were still on the run. One evening as the three of us were crossing an almost deserted place, I heard a noise coming from the bushes. Pointing my gun, I shouted, "Qui vive!" As an answer, bullets came our way. Throwing ourselves on the ground, I started shooting. A cry told us I had hit someone … someone who was also running away. A search the next day found the German wounded in the thigh.

The German pianist was a well-known musician in Germany and he begged me to help take him away from his other assignment, which was digging in the mines. He was afraid of damaging his hands. Upon my request, they all agreed and kept him as a musician and toilet keeper.

The officers' quarters were in Hyeres itself in a nice hotel, Avenue Gambetta, which was used for Army officers only. They had given me a large room with a toilet. It was a half-hour walk from the barracks every night. Thornton was afraid for my safety and gave me another 45. "Too many Senegalais around," he used to say, although they were the ones who gave me the least amount of problems … if none at all.

I had given Thornton the signal for me to let him in my room: two long knocks and two short ones. He was careful trying not to be seen, but he must have, because the attitude of my fellow Army officers changed. I didn't care. I was so much in love with my handsome American Staff Sergeant. He was married I knew, but ready to divorce because of her infidelity. His friend, Gordon, had been the translator. Thornton was ten years older than I was and had no children. He had his own butcher shop in Turlock, California.

A dance in honor of the American and French Armies had been prepared at the Town Hall. Although the fighting was still going on not far away, Hyeres had been liberated. It was a very special evening. The music was mostly Glenn Miller, mixed with French songs. The place was full and jumping. I was always dancing with Thornton who was trying to teach me the jive. A Frenchman who had unsuccessfully asked me to dance before, came back again to cut in—this time with an attitude and drunk.

"Allez, on dance." "No," I said, "Merci." Qu'est ce c'est, les Francais sont pas assez bon?" he said, taking me by the arm. (What, the French are not good enough?) That is when Thornton intervened.

"Hey, what's going on?"

"La ferme, Amerlo." (Shut up, American!)

Towering over him, Thornton pushed him backward—that's when the fight started—American vs. French, until the MPs came in and put a stop to it. What a mess! Yet, I'll always remember that day with great amusement and nostalgia. We were young and foolish.

It's also about this time that the Colonel called me into his office and confronted me with a letter he had received from someone from Le Lavandou objecting to my being in the Army after having been 'friendly' with a German. I did not deny it. Not wanting to put the Colonel in the difficult position of firing me, I resigned. He was a wonderful man and I will always be grateful to him for hiring me and trusting me. Life is a pay-off deal—you screw up, you pay eventually. Strange as it may seem, I have no regrets.

Being with Thornton was lots of fun. One day he decided to go up the hill in his jeep. Going too fast, we almost tilted below. If that was not enough, he and his friend decided to target practice in the woods and it caught fire. While stationed in Hyeres, he and the American soldiers were living at Villa Bocage, a lovely home. The homeowners had happily lent it to the Americans for as long as they would need it.

One day, the Americans were celebrating Thanksgiving and invited us to a typical American Thanksgiving dinner. Cranberry sauce served with turkey was very new to me and the other French girls, who were guests that day as well. It was also the same day that the disappearance of Glenn Miller over the Atlantic was big news. A great loss!

When Thornton and his battalion left for Paris, I took Grandma shopping in Toulon. We were only there for an hour when the sirens started their warnings. "Here we go again, Grandma." Our shopping trip ended inside a bomb shelter. It was a bad one, but the last one for Toulon. Many died that day. However, it was also the last bombing we personally would experience in the war. We almost suffocated in the shelter.

Shortly after Thornton's departure, I decided to go to Paris. At the request of my uncle, my stepfather's mother agreed to lodge me in her townhouse in Neuilly. My paternal family was still in hiding.

Paris

adame de Rieux Depaux received me as well as expected with her very limited warmth. She let me have one of the maid's rooms, which was empty, since she had only kept one live-in maid. Her townhouse in Neuilly was gorgeous inside and out. She was still a beautiful woman, but cold, and had spent a fortune on her looks. I felt my presence there was a nuisance to her and she was only repaying my uncle for a past favor he had done for her. She asked me to help Justine, the maid, which I did readily. She had a room full of furs, such as mink, chinchilla, and Russian sable, eleven in all. I believe in order to teach me 'humility' and to show me her importance, she decided to put me in charge of her furs. This chore consisted of bringing them into the garden twice a week, weather permitting, hanging them up on a rope, then beating them up with a stick for five minutes each, just to keep their skin healthy and breathing. Arrogance and jealousy on her part perhaps. She might have been rich, but I was young and pretty—nature's irreplaceable gift.

Being short of clothes, I found one of Mme de Rieux's old dresses in the attic, with a gold/pearl pin attached. She had mentioned old clothes in the attic that were to be given away. I should have asked her, but left to see Thornton. When I returned, she was waiting for me. "You stole my dress."

"No, I only borrowed it, you weren't here to ask." What she didn't know was I gave the pin to Thornton as a souvenir. "I'll tell your uncle to find you another place."

By luck, my paternal family, Aunt Linda and Aunt Yvonne, were back from hiding. I stayed in an apartment where my Aunt Linda owned the building, Avenue Victor Hugo.

I had what I believed must have been a miscarriage then. I was bleeding a lot for three days. Although some fighting was still going on, the war was almost over. To this day I still don't know how I came out alive. As the song goes, "It was written in the stars."

Thornton was stationed outside of Paris in a big castle, where we had met many times before. I remember one of my last meetings with Thornton in Paris. It was a beautiful day and we were walking. When I stopped and kissed him on the lips, he smiled and said, "You know, you could not do that in America."

I understood him. I thought, "Gee, it must be their Puritan upbringing." Even though I'm now 85, I remember the dress he bought me that day: navy and white polka dots. How great the souvenir, but it was also our last night of love. How I loved my handsome American. Although marriage was not mentioned, we promised to stay in touch and in love. The week before, he had introduced me to his brother, a friendly, nice guy who also was being shipped back after serving in Europe.

When Thornton left for America, my heart was broken. I had renewed my friendship with Albert Taylor, who was also stationed in Paris, because I had a scheme in mind. Albert was a temporary student at the Sorbonne while still in the Army. He was a nice decent man who spoke French, which was a big plus. I liked him, but did not love him.

In the meantime, my Aunt Linda had introduced me to a very wealthy Frenchman whom she wanted me to marry. But I was in love. The armistice finally arrived April 29, 1945. The Germans had surrendered and Hitler committed suicide. Bon Voyage!

Albert Taylor proposed to me and I accepted with one thing in mind—being near Thornton. Unfair? Yes, I should have told him my reason for accepting his proposal. Better yet, I shouldn't have married him. A few days before my marriage to Albert, I had spent with Thornton, our last lovemaking.

My grandma and uncle came to see me get married. Albert requested a church wedding. I wore a navy blue suit and an unhappy heart. Our wedding night was a disaster—I feigned a stomach ache. The hotel where we stayed was very old and so was the hallway toilet, which was a hole in the ground and a handle to hold onto. Albert was unfamiliar with such facilities, so he misjudged his footing and his right foot got stuck in the hole. It took him a good ten minutes to get his leg out and what came with it. He was swearing in English as he came back into the room trying to clean himself up inside the small sink that was there. Between my laughter and his humiliation, we called it a night. I continually found excuses to avoid his love making as often as possible. Yet, shortly afterward, I found myself pregnant.

The time came for us to go to the United States. On his last day at Sorbonne, while waiting in line at the canteen, someone stole my wallet with all my Army papers in it. To this day, it upsets me. My paternal uncle, Leon Schiffers, helped me get my legal papers so I could follow my husband back to the States as a war bride. My Uncle Leon bribed one of the agents to speed up the process.

Albert had left two months earlier. When it came my turn

to leave on the *Vulcania,* my grandmother's heart broke. Leaving France, my family and especially my grandmother was hard. But my goal was, or so I thought, to be with Thornton again. (*Oh, what a tangled web we weave when we first practice to deceive.*)

Prior to embarking on our designated ship, all the war brides were assigned into different camps by the Army: Camp Camel, Chesterfield, Lucky Strike, just to name a few. I was assigned Camp Lucky Strike, where we all shared dormitories, like soldiers. The facilities were under a tent. In the center stood two large circular wooden tables, each adorned with ten toilet seats to used as needed, where needed. No privacy and embarrassing, to say the least.

If that was not enough, one day when another bride and I were using the seats, I heard a noise. Turning around I saw the tent moving. Someone was watching us. Taking our pants, we ran out calling security. It turned out to be German prisoners, whose chores were to clean the toilets, but they had made a hole in the tent so they could watch us as we went 'potty.'

Finally we were boarding the *Vulcania,* a fairly big ship. I shared a cabin with three other girls: one black girl, Josephine, was going to Harlem, Genevieve was bound for Detroit and Anne to Georgia, but I was the only one pregnant. We all became friends and were on our way to America like millions before us. We made a stop in Southampton, England before we left Europe.

The first couple of days went fairly well, but as the sea started acting up, so did my stomach. Lemons and crackers are supposed to be good, so I gave the steward $2.00 and he brought me some. I stayed in bed much of that long trip: 21 days at sea. The sea was never my cup of tea, since my father had drowned and that didn't help, nor did my being pregnant. The *Vulcania* finally arrived in New York. Thank God!

I said goodbye to my newly made friends and promised to keep in touch. Albert was there waiting with his friend, Richard, who was a writer for Esquire Magazine and who had been a war buddy of Albert.

After Richard had taken our picture, we went our separate ways, toward the unknown, toward our destiny, hoping for the best. However, before going to Boston, Albert and Richard decided to show me a little of New York With Richard as our driver. What a thrill! So this was America! The America I fell in love with while watching American movies with my grandma. It was everything I dreamed of and more. The buildings were so tall and impressive. We stopped to eat at Horn & Hardart, which I found most unusual and lots of fun—sticking coins in a hole for food in return! Only in America!

Finally, Richard took us back to where Albert had parked his own car. After saying goodbye to Richard, hoping to see him again, Albert and I were on our way to my new life in Boston. My feelings on the way there were mixed. The scenery was sheer delight, but every once in a while, my mind kept going back to the child I was carrying. What if … ?

We finally arrived at our destination, Albert's father's house, which we were going to share with Albert's two widowed sisters, Kathryn and Gertrude. Their Irish mother had died two years earlier. It was a modest two-story house located in a quiet lovely neighborhood in West Roxbury, a Boston suburb. The second floor was rented to two pleasant elderly ladies.

Albert and I were given the downstairs room, which they had transformed into a bedroom and added a crib. These, of course, were temporary accommodations, until we could find a house.

Adapting was not easy, especially when the language is foreign. His family was friendly, but Albert accused me of being stuck-up—perhaps from my upbringing. My blunders were numerous, so what was funny to me became Custer's last stand to Albert, Anglo-Saxon prudery versus Gallic mischievousness. My in-laws must have thought that Albert had lost his marbles. I was 20 years younger and couldn't speak English. They were a very Catholic family and I was mixed, Jewish and Catholic. When asked, I always answered, "I believe in God." My new family really didn't know what to make of me.

Albert's father, Alfred, was a tall, good-looking, strict man and the only one with a sense of humor. He was born in England. Whenever I did something 'naughty,' I would see a twinkle in his eyes and a smile on his lips. His children did not especially like him, but I did. Their extremely religious Irish mother had been the one they really liked.

Albert had very few friends, of whom David O'Brady was one. When seated next to him, you could hear the strong beating of his heart—weird. Living at my father-in-law's house was not a comfortable situation, on both sides. For me, it was also a lonely time. Our social life was slow, since he was not an outgoing person, while our sex life was non-existent— my fault, because he was not the warmest person either. In France, we would have jokingly characterized him as 'constipated.' As I look back, I deeply regret my actions. Albert was a good and decent man, but we were 100% wrong for each other. We both had married for the wrong reasons. He married me for my looks and I married him to be near Thornton, so we both were screwed! He knew I didn't love him and that I just wanted to come to America. However, the real reason I found out was that he wanted to stay in France, but I refused. Although financially, I was better off over there in France. On my behalf, I must admit that I liked Albert and respected him. Of course, as in every marriage, good or bad, life goes on …

Albert had his teaching job and I stayed home waiting for him to return and be my translator. My English left very much to be desired.

In the meantime, the baby was growing in my body. I had a very good doctor and I couldn't wait to give birth. Morning sicknesses were pretty bad. How I missed my grandma, whom heartbreakingly, I was never to see again. Strangely enough, I didn't regret leaving Europe, because I loved America.

My feelings for Thornton were starting to cool off. Obviously he didn't care.

Albert introduced me to some nice friends at church—very proper, very Bostonian. I decided to invite them for a lovely dinner. I wanted this to be very special and to show off my culinary talent (which I thought I had) and also make Albert proud. After all I owed him something. I had decided to make a chicken as a main course. My sister-in-law, Gertrude, offered to help, but I refused. In order to leave us alone to entertain, my in-laws decided to spend the evening with Albert's other married sister, Cecilia.

Everything was ready, including me, in time to receive our friends, Linda and George Williams and Jane and Walter

O'Neill, who came in on schedule, bringing lovely flowers. We exchanged greetings both in French and English. They spoke about how hot and scorching the day was. So I tried some English. "Hot! Very hot! A douche is good." Only what I didn't know was that 'douche' in English has a very different meaning; which in French means a *shower*. Poor Albert was trying to translate douche to four frozen people with their mouths open.

I asked, "Qu'est-ce-que J'ai' dit?" (What did I say?) "Plus tard," (later) was his response while sponging his face. "Cocktails?" I asked smiling. Four heads shook yes simultaneously! Cocktails were Albert's department. Everybody did relax after the second one. I don't care, but there is still a lot to be said about booze. Anyway, less uptight now, our friends tried using the few French words they knew; while I in return tried using the little English I had picked up making Albert a nervous wreck.

Then came time to eat. To make a good impression, I had set a lovely dining room table, which they seemed to like, since the word, lovely, which I understood, was mentioned many times. I had brought in the hors d'oeuvres that everyone seemed to be enjoying except for Jane, whom I noticed was missing a fork. That's when again I very proudly tried my English. "Oh, Jane! You need a 'fuck.' Ignoring the sudden silence in the room, proud of myself, I repeated,

"Albert, please give Jane a fuck." I turned to Albert whose face had suddenly turned scarlet. Everyone there sat frigid, their mouths open as in deja' vue. Albert stood up and spoke rapidly. Which as he later explained to me was an apology for my *mispronunciation* of the word, 'fork.' Jane seemed in complete shock. George started giggling, but stopped at the severe look he received from his wife.

Walter took the wine bottle and helped himself. Obviously, I again had made a boo-boo. The atmosphere was a little strained by then. As I brought in the chicken, I decided to give my English a rest. The chicken looked really nice until Albert cut it open and exposed all the guts and such the chicken had when still alive. Albert's face turned from red to white and once more, as all through our marriage, he spoke his famous line, "J'aurais du me faire Curé." (I should have been a priest.) The salad was too salty, the mashed potatoes had lumps and the cake was burnt. The limburger cheese stood there alone too smelly for American taste—*quel désastre!* (disastrous) Thank God for the wine. Like I said before, booze has its own reward. Our friends seemed to walk faster on their way out than they did on their way in. Albert never let me forget that day and it will always stay engraved in my mind, if only the comical side of it, as I recall the absolute shock on the faces of those lovely ladies upon the mention of 'fuck.'

On July 21st, the childbirth pains started and lasted for 16 hours. Albert reproached me for not waiting for my water to break before leaving for the hospital. How did I know? I never had a child before! It was a very hard childbirth, which required many stitches to close the opening they needed to make. The incision stayed painful most of my life. He was a beautiful baby boy, 8 pounds, 10 ounces -- He was all Thornton. I never let Thornton know he had a son. Albert suspected it, mostly due to his lack of resemblance to the boy, whom we named Brian.

When the baby was two months old, a very strange incident happened. Albert and I had a fight, so he decided to sleep upstairs while I stayed downstairs with the baby. During the middle of the night, I woke up. Half-asleep, half-awake, I saw a small shining light coming from the stairs to the right where the crib was located. As I lay there motionless, I saw the figure of my mother walking slowly down the stairs. She then stopped at my son's crib, bent down and gave him a kiss. I wanted to go to her and ask her many questions, but I was unable to move or speak. She then stood up, looked at me almost like giving us her blessing and slowly went back upstairs, all dressed in black. It was so unbelievably real that to this day I can still feel her 'ghost' coming to see us. I never told my husband, who would only have laughed at me or mentioned 'demons.' He was an extremely strong Christian with very old beliefs.

There are also certain things that are better left untold.

We never had many fights. I don't believe in them and would walk away rather than make a scene. Going to church after the baby was born had become a problem. Sitting on a wooden bench for two hours was extremely painful for me, because of my stitches. However, Albert felt that I should ignore my pains in the name of God. Well! I was never a saint, so after sitting as long as I could, I would leave and walk back home alone.

He felt that it was his duty to stay. His father was always outraged. Albert's excuse: My father is an Episcopalian.

Aside from visiting Boston, which I loved, and its environment and occasional movies, our social life was practically non-existent. Albert was right—he should have been a priest.

One of my last boo-boo's at my father-in-law's house was a beaut!

I had a doctor's appointment that day and was asked to bring a urine sample. I had Albert ask Gertrude for a jar. After the test was done, the nurse gave me back the jar. When I returned home, I cleaned and sterilized it and put it back on the shelf in the pantry. Albert and I were playing with Brian in the living room when all of a sudden, a cry of horror came from the kitchen. Before we could go find out what it was about, Gertrude flew in brandishing that same jar. Her English was too fast for me to understand, but I got the picture anyway.

It was Albert's turn to speak, "Why on earth did you put this thing back on the shelf?" I couldn't understand what all the fuss was about, as I explained, "I thought Gertrude wanted it back, so I cleaned and sterilized it." As he translated it, he and his sisters looked absolutely shocked, "It's not the thing to do," he said. "It's terrible, absolutely unheard of, undignified and shameful!" Everything to Albert was shameful. Only my father-in-law was giggling, which got him a 'How dare you?' stare from his children. I then apologized, "Excusez-moi," as I took the jar and threw it away.

That did it for Albert who went house hunting the next day. He didn't have to look very far. On the next street over, Redlands Road, he found an imposing two-story Deca house (two-story row home). He bought it under the GI Bill of Rights for $17,000, which was a lot of money then. The downstairs flat was already rented out and Albert wanted those people, a couple and their mother, to move upstairs. But I refused. Why? To this day ,I don't know. "l'esprit de contradictions," I guess. (spirit of contradictions) We bought furniture and moved upstairs. Although Albert was a decent man and trying his best to be a fine husband, for me, doing the right thing in those days was not in my dictionary. However, it did go well for some time, since more privacy and liberty helped. I remember our first refrigerator was a Kelvinator. Had I been smart, I would have tried making the best of things and be grateful, if only for just being alive.

I loved my child, but not the motherly duties. I had too many fires burning inside me. Away from my family and friends, not being able to speak English and obviously having lost the man I loved—God's punishment—it wasn't long (maybe a year) before I had a nervous breakdown. I was in such bad shape, Albert had to call a doctor in the middle of the night. I was screaming and carrying on, so the doctor gave me morphine. Albert thought I was dying and called the priest, who gave me the Last Rites. This happened three times in the following months. I didn't dare face our downstairs tenants who had heard the commotion. They probably were wondering why on earth did that nice guy marry that crazy French girl. "Never judge someone until you have walked a mile in their moccasins."

Whenever mad at me, Albert always threw my Jewish heritage in my face, which I resented a great deal. One day, I decided no more breakdowns, but that I would take my life in hand and use all the strength left in me. I also continued fighting anxiety and the fear of illness, which has followed me all my life since my mother's death. I continued writing to my grandma and whenever possible, called her on the phone. In those days, it was a big deal to make or receive a phone call.

We had a three-party line: one ring was for party #1, 2 rings for party #2, and 3 rings were for us. Of course, privacy was non-existent, so making a phone call was difficult. You picked up the receiver and someone was almost always on the line. We had to wait until they hung up to make our call. To find out if the line was free, we had to pick up the phone and listen again. That was a pain in the ass for all the parties concerned and tempers flared up more than once upon accusations of eavesdropping. That used to enrage Albert.

I was taking better care of the house than before, watching and playing with Brian more enthusiastically and my English was getting better. Then when Brian was two-years-old, my uncle sent a telegram that my grandma was dying and asking for me. I asked Albert for two tickets, so I could take Brian, whom she would love to see. First he agreed, but then changed his mind three days prior to the trip, which was very difficult for me. My grandma passed away one month later, still asking for me. The one person who really loved me had died. How I missed her—I still do.

That's when I decided to change my life completely, to start working and make my own money. I always loved music and for some time now, I had in mind to become a singer. I was brought up with music, mostly opera and operetta, since my mother was a trained opera singer. but had never performed in front of an audience.

As a child I used to play my "Master's Voice" phonograph and sing along with the records almost every day. I remembered my mother telling me, "La Diction, bébé, La Diction." This she said, along with 'feelings', were the most important things for a singer,. after the voice and the pitch. I had no difficulty in the voice and looks department, so only the technique was missing.

I remember one day when the rodeo was in town, Gene Autry was the star. Albert was given two tickets, so we went. I loved the show. After it ended, I asked Albert to go backstage to ask for his autograph. He finally agreed and we met Gene Autry. Noticing my accent, he asked Albert where I came from. He said he was giving a party that night and invited us. But Albert, noticing his interest in me, didn't accept. That made me sick! He seemed like a very interesting man.

The glamour and the love of Gene Autry's fans reinforced my desire to be in show business. I used to stand in front of the mirror, singing and think, "Gee, I know I've got it, but it doesn't come out right somehow." It's one thing loving to sing and another being able to deliver a song. I had heard about a studio and decided to give it a try, over Albert's objections.

By then I was doing quite well in English, so I enrolled in evening classes in voice, but I was not very good at learning from books and teaching. I needed more experience, which I ended up getting later on anyway. After a week of classes,

I knew it wasn't for me. There was a student named Eddy who had been a Marine and was attending on a GI Bill. A nice-looking, dark skinned Portuguese, a decent young man. He had a wonderful voice, and a great sense of rhythm and phrasing, immense talent. An important manager was interested in handling him, but due to Eddy's lack of drive and self-confidence, he switched and handled Steve Lawrence instead. It amazed me to see someone with so much talent, but so little ambition, although he loved to sing. When he performed on the stage as he did later, the public loved him. He was very helpful to me with rhythm and phrasing. One of our teachers told him, "If you only had the drive and ambition that Jacqueline has, you'd be a star."

Well, we became lovers. My husband had pretty much given up, but was still trying to hold on to me. This is a part of my life, I deeply regret. As I look back, I see that I was not a very good woman, since my life was mostly about me, myself and I. I had looked for an apartment and finally found one on Beacon Street at $35 a month, a bargain. The woman owner seemed to like me. I remember with great regret and shame the time I had to tell Albert that I was leaving. He was not a man of violent reactions. I still see him with hurt in his eyes, telling me to think about Brian, whom he was holding in his arms. I can still see my little boy looking at me when I left. I must have been a hell of a bitch in those days, or perhaps, heartless would be a better word. However, I can say that you do pay later on in life for all the wrongs you've done. My poor husband was better off without me, but I can still see, as I left, my little boy with his hand in his mouth, not understanding, but feeling what was going on. How could I? It was unforgivable and my conscience, which I acquired later on, made sure of that. After this, Albert refused to let me see Brian, but finally agreed, only if he were allowed to stay with us during my visit. I was in such a mess in those days, I didn't know what to do.

I was pushing Eddy and helped him get some good singing dates. But many a time he would find an excuse for not accepting the booking. I never asked for financial help from Albert. I felt that it wouldn't have been fair—I had some decency left in me after all—so I found myself a booking agent. I knew a few songs, mostly French, which luckily were popular right after the war. My first job was in an upscale club, where I had to sing two songs. The MC was friendly and asked how I wanted to be introduced, but I told him that it was up to him. An old timer, sax player, let me in on tricks singers use before going on the stage, "Always look at your audience first before deciding what song to sing." A small hole had been made in the curtain for that purpose. "Their mood should tell you what song to sing," he added. Right now, my problem was facing an audience. The MC had already announced my name as the next act. "And now ladies and gentlemen, coming to us directly from France, is a girl who fought her way through the war right into our hearts, the lovely Jacqueline Jourdan." (A stage name I had given myself.) Well, guess what? Like my mother, I had stage fright and stood there frozen in my beautiful red lace dress, hiding behind the curtain. "OK FRENCHIE, you're on." When the band started the opening bars of my intro, I realized that no enemy had ever sent such chills through me. The MC's earlier friendliness had given way to a strictly business attitude, so after his second call, he came behind me and said, "Let's go, Frenchie." Then with his foot gave me a push on my derriere, sending me flying onto the stage where I landed on my ass.

People were laughing hysterically. As I picked myself up, the MC handed me the mike with one word, "Sing!" Meanwhile the orchestra started giving my cue again. The lights were blinding me. "Just as well," I thought, "I won't see their faces that way." Clearing my throat, with a stupid smile on my face, I started "J'attendrai." "Oops, I'm in the wrong key. "Le jour et la nuit," "Oops, too low." More laughs. "J'attendrai toujours." Finally, I was in pitch. "That's the girl, Frenchie." (I was starting to hate that word.) "You got it! You can't sing that great, but you're some dish." Then came my big finish with the song, "Ton retour." Thank God! "Hey, you made it." I stood there soaking wet with perspiration. "More,

more!" they yelled. I was a novelty. My voice was more than adequate and so was my appearance, so I got away with it. My second song went OK, but the closing star act that day was the Sammy Davis Trio, a blessing for the audience. Later on, someone said, "You're like a diamond still in its original creation." Another lady was less flattering and said, "She's got nerve, who does she think she is?" she snapped. Whatever I had, I went through with it, with more guts than talent.

The rest came later on with work and experience. I must not have done too badly, since job offers started to come in. However, as I said before, at the time, I was a novelty act and they couldn't wait to see more of Frenchie making a fool of herself again, landing on her butt while singing off-key, my agent told me. But that didn't happen, as I started getting much better as I kept working. I was doing my American songs by then, which helped me a great deal and I started watching the well-known singers of that time on TV, such as Peggy Lee, Lena Horne, and Dinah Shore. I borrowed some of their tricks and added some of my own. I also made sure to look the best I could onstage. I always felt that we owed our public not only to sing our best, but also to present a striking appearance. If you want to look like a slob, stay home and sing in the toilet. By then, I was ahead in my career and even joined the American Guild of Variety Artists (AGVA) union. If you hadn't paid your dues, their agents were there to collect after you sang. Eddy was also doing a few club dates and joined the union.

Then like a fool, I got pregnant. I worked as long as I could. We lived on his club dates and office work. Somehow we survived and had a handsome baby boy, but again, the delivery was not easy. The hospital was not nearly as welcoming or qualified as the last one, so I ended up with a very painful dysentery. When this was over, I decided that I would go to New York where jobs were more abundant. The baby was named Stephen and we made arrangements with Eddy's brother and his wife to keep Stephen until we could get settled in New York. They agreed for a price, so I also left all my clothes at their house, which they eventually sold without my knowledge. Sadly, I had to leave Stephen behind.

When I arrived in New York, I contacted some friends of my father's family who lived on Park Avenue. They were very nice, but when they found out about Eddy, they refused to recommend their theatrical contacts. We found an apartment in Greenwich Village and I started contacting talent agencies for both of us. Of course, his excuses for not working were numerous. His teeth needed fixing. An agent impressed by his talent and appearance had them fixed. He managed then to keep his club dates for six months, until we had to move in a hurry, in the middle of the night for lack of payment. He had spent the money, so we moved in with some of his friends for two weeks before moving to West 49th Street.

By then I was working steadily and sending money for Stephen. I was making more and more friends in show business. Albert contacted me, because he wanted to sell the house and needed my signature. I met him in Boston, where I was finally reunited with Brian, if only for two days—it was wonderful and painful at the same time. I returned to New York with the promise to be back soon. Albert was cold as expected, but he gave me my share from the sale of the house.

Eddy and I moved to West 69th Street, where I obtained a divorce. However, because of a malfunction in a condom, I was pregnant again. That was the last straw! I was sick of the whole situation, sick of him and his laziness.

While singing on W. 52nd Street, I had made friends with a fine, good-looking and wealthy man named Jack, who took a liking to me. After becoming aware of my situation, he decided to help me financially. We started seeing each other and Eddy was disappearing more and more.

One day while at home, there was a knock on the door. Two men came in and asked for Eddy, who as usual, wasn't home. They were detectives who wanted to know where Eddy had been the day before. I didn't know and told them so. I wanted to know why. "Because," one of the men answered, "someone he knew was murdered and then robbed. He was one of the last individuals to visit that man." I nearly fainted. They left with the promise to be back.

When Eddy came home, I confronted him. He admitted having been with the man in question, but had nothing to do with his murder. He also admitted receiving money from him for some favor he had done for him, but refused to tell me what kind. His association with this person was very strange and left a lot to be desired.

By then, I'd really had enough! When my pretty baby girl was born, my new friend, Jack had helped me to find a good doctor and hospital. I named the baby, Leslie Anne. Eddy wanted me to put the baby up for adoption, which I absolutely refused to do. Then his brother refused to keep Stephen any longer, so I sent Eddy to bring Stephen back to me. Stephen was sickly and had obviously not been taken care of as well as he should have been.

Jack found me a new apartment on E. 33rd Street and although I was finished with Eddy, I still shared the apartment with him, so he could take care of the children while I worked. Then one day, a friend of mine introduced me to a very pleasant lady who was going back to France to visit her parents in Thionville where they owned a house. They also occasionally took care of children and were looking for two more since their last two had gone back to their parents. I became interested and after my inquiries and speaking on the phone with the people, I found them very trustworthy and enjoyable. It was an occasion for Steve and Leslie Anne not only to learn French, but also be in better surroundings. At the same time, this enabled me to get rid of Eddy who wanted to 'see' Europe. After agreeing on a monthly tuition fee with Mr. and Mrs. Ramirez, I financed the trip on a ship for the children and Eddy. The couple's daughter and husband were traveling on the same ship and would keep an eye on the children, which made me feel much better. They would all meet upon arrival. Everything went as planned and the children enjoyed the trip, while Eddy went his own way in Sweden looking for bookings. Instead, eventually found a woman with money and married her, leaving me with a $700 phone bill. He also took the cash I had put aside, so I sold my old engagement ring to obtain much-needed money. Thank God for his leaving and finding someone else. Toward the end, he had become violent and very jealous. I was left with the financial care of the children, but it was well worth it. I also had decided to keep Jack only as a friend.

Soon after that, my luck began changing and I started making important friends. I then appeared in famous nightclubs both in and out of the U.S. I hired the very talented Bobby Kroll to do my special material and orchestrations. I was sponsored by Don Spencer, who owned an advertising agency on Madison Ave. His daughter, Diane Spencer, had recently co-starred with Jerry Lewis in a motion picture.

Somewhere around that time, I received a call from a man I didn't know, who told me, "There is a car outside your apartment. It's a Ferrari and it's yours. I'd like to take you out to dinner tonight." After the initial shock, I asked, "Who are you and how did you get my phone number, when it's not listed?"

"Oh, we have our ways," he stated flatly, so I hung up abruptly. Indeed, there was such a car outside. Of course, my first reaction was, here goes another nut. The next day, I received the same call. I started feeling queasy about this whole affair. Again I asked his name, but he wouldn't tell me.

"Did you like the car?" he said. "There is much more of whatever you want if you say 'yes,'" he insisted. "Sir," I said, "Don't call me anymore." "My name is Anastasia," he finally said. "I heard you sing and you're pretty talented. I'll call you tomorrow."

This was weird. I spoke to some friends about the calls. "Siri," my dearest girlfriend, a showgirl from Sweden asked, "Did you say, Anastasia?" I answered, "Yeah."

"Are you sure?" she insisted. "That's the name he gave me." She looked shocked. "Well, my dear friend, he is the Boss of the Gambino Crime Family of the Mafia." (He was known as the Chief Executioner of Murder.) It was my turn to be in shock. "Are you sure?" I finally asked. "Oh, yeah." I think I said, "Oh shit!"

I must admit the temptation for all the goodies was pretty strong, but I had heard about being at the wrong place at the wrong time. In this case, it could have been being with the wrong person and possibly being gunned down. After all, this was the top guy who, I was sure, had many enemies. So the next time he called, I said, "No, thank you," but I had to repeat myself many times later, because he was very persistent. Many of my girlfriends had Mafia boyfriends and they were known to be the most generous. However, Anastasia was the top man and, therefore, the danger would be worse with him. Since I had already had enough dangers earlier in my life, I was probably overly cautious, but war and experience had taught me to keep away from eventual trouble. On October 25, 1957, Albert Anastasia was gunned down in a barber's chair, while having a shave at the Park Sheraton Hotel in New York City.

I was introduced to a great woman, Julia Skouras, the co-owner of 20th Century Fox movies. She had taken a liking to me and said I reminded her of her daughter who had committed suicide in Italy. She invited me to be part of the Italian Centennial Ball for the Boys Towns of Italy. It was a very chic affair and I performed as an entertainer. Among the committee were Lyndon B. Johnson, Nelson A. Rockefeller, and Clare Boothe Luce, just to name a few.

Julia was a wonderful woman, who wanted to introduce

me into acting and motion pictures. She passed away rather unexpectedly, which was a terrible loss for many, but it was an especially terrible loss for me, spiritually and career-wise.

During one of my star personality appearances on the ship, SS President Monroe anchored in New York, I met its Captain, Earl Evans.

At this time, the French Consul was promoting, Nuits-Saint-Georges, an expensive French wine. Captain Evans and I fell madly in love and had a torrid affair. He had been unhappy in his marriage for many years, so we saw each other whenever his ship was in town. For a long time I had wanted to visit my children, Stephen and Leslie Anne, so we made plans to meet in Europe. I flew to France and had a wonderful time with my children. I was very satisfied with their environment.

Next, I left for Marseille, where I boarded Earl's ship and cruised to Italy. His ship's port of call was in Florence, so we anchored for just a few days, enough to visit Florence and Portofino. It was beautiful in every way. Earl was a tall, distinguished, good-looking man who adored me. He bought me a beautiful sapphire and diamond clasp for my pearl necklace. I will always cherish it.

Back home, whenever he could, he would travel to see my show. We had two perfect years, but for some reason I am still trying to understand, my feelings for him cooled off. On his next vacation, he went home to San Francisco to ask his wife for a divorce. For two weeks, I waited to hear from him. When he came back, I broke up with him. He had spent his time getting her to agree to a divorce, my decision devastated him. After begging me for more than a week to change my mind, he went back home to San Francisco and shot himself. His friend, Captain Kindnawaiser, called me and told me of his death. It was terrible, a deep-seated guilt to carry around for the rest of my life. He was buried at sea, as he had requested. I will always love and pray for him. I am so sorry.

Once again, I had lost someone I loved.

I started thinking again about Thornton, so I decided to look for his name in the phone book and to my surprise, it was listed. I debated for a few days about calling him, but finally I did. He answered and I nearly fainted at the sound of his voice. We spoke in English for the first time. He was thrilled to hear from me and told me he had tried to find me, but was unsuccessful. He found out that all the letters I sent him had been destroyed by his mother. He was now in the midst of another divorce and had two daughters. In respect for Albert, I never told him about Brian. We exchanged addresses. He told me his brother had died of a heart attack last year.

I had a contract to sing on the *SS Argentina*, which was going to South America for over a month, so we made plans to meet upon my return. We were both so happy. The *SS Argentina* was great and had only one class, luxury. Another singer was on the ship, Harold Lloyd, Jr., the son of the famous comedian and we made friends immediately. He was a very agreeable young man, lots of fun, and very friendly, who, after a week, asked me to marry him. Of course, I said, "No."

When the ship stopped in Trinidad we all went ashore. The dancers, the MC, and the musicians all got stoned. Harold jumped into the water with his new extremely expensive watch, Patek Philippe which was ruined.

Then halfway to Brazil, we hit a typhoon. Many of the passengers including myself, were very sick. I was on the stage when it began. I remember holding on to the mike, while the bottles and glasses were falling on the floor. Scary!!!! Very scary!

We stopped in Argentina and did the tango in a fantastic nightclub, which had a circular stage that brought on new musicians each half hour. However, we were not well received and the audience kept shouting, "Go home, Yankees!"

When we finally headed back to the ship, we were caught in crossfire. Buenos Aires was in the middle of a mini-revolution. I remember we tried to avoid the bullets by hiding on the floor of the bus-like car, while praying that the driver would not get hit. Sort of deja vu—again!

Finally, our ship arrived in Brazil a few days later. We all had a great time. Harold and I went shopping for jewelry for at $35.00-an-ounce for gold in those days, it was a buyer's paradise. We toured many of the nightclubs, but I was only allowed to sing aboard ship, which made it more of a vacation for me than work. I bought myself a beautiful Tourmaline ring (South American emerald).

Then came time to go back home. Some of our passengers had disembarked, while others joined us. The return was quieter and a little sad. Harold and I kept in touch for a long time and he invited me to his family's mansion in California. I also kept in touch with many of those passengers.

I do remember with melancholy all of us being baptized while passing through the Southern Cross on our way to Brazil.

But nothing could be compared to the thrill I felt at the thought of seeing Thornton again—I couldn't wait to get home. I went through all my mail, but not one letter was from him. I did not call since he had my number and it was his turn. I thought I should have known better. Three days later, the phone rang in the morning. A woman asked, "Jacqueline?" "Yes, speaking." She cleared her voice. "This is Ella, Ella Goodin." "Oh, yes," I said, "you are Thornton's sister-in-law." "Yes," she said and started crying. I froze! A terrible feeling had suddenly taken hold of me. "What's wrong?" I could barely speak. She was sobbing. "What's wrong?" I repeated, afraid of the answer.

Finally she spoke the terrible news. "Thornton is dead, a heart attack." "NO!" I screamed. "No! Why?"

She told me that he had died two weeks ago and she was waiting for me to come back. He had fallen sick and told her to let me know that he'd come to me as soon as he could. He died not knowing he had a son. The pain was excruciating. He had been my first big love. We had just found each other again, only to be separated, this time forever. It just wasn't fair. Life, that Magnificent Bitch, had done it to me again. It took me a long time for me to overcome this tragedy. I went to see Ella, who took me to his grave. We corresponded until she, herself, passed away a few years later.

It was some time before I went back on the stage. When I finally did, it was a big healer. I sang at the Sheraton-Blackstone in Chicago, where I worked in radio and TV with Bobby Darin. I met Bob Hope at the Shamrock-Hilton in Houston, TX. Always in search of talent, he had come to catch my show. What a thrill! He was a lovely, friendly man, with lots of class. I was invited to his party that evening. He even offered me a small part in one of his movies, which I couldn't accept, because of previous engagements that I couldn't break.

My next engagement was in Montreal at the Ritz Carlton. There I met Tony Bennett and Gary Morton, who were working at another club in Montreal. After our shows, I went to Tony's apartment with Gary and cooked pasta. I dated Gary for a while, but his pot smoking turned me off. He later married Lucille Ball.

From there I sang at Little Bay Hotel in St. Martin, Hotel Intercontinental in Curacao (Cave de Neptune), Hotel El Embajador in Santo Domingo and the Statler Hotel in Buffalo. I had sung before in that city at a small club. At that time, they gave me a hard time and were even rude. The funny thing is that I came back at the Hilton as a star. Life is funny. I also performed at the New York Statler Hotel (Café Rouge), the Palace Hotel in Surinam, the Old New Orleans in Washington, DC and Hotel Aruba Caribbean in Aruba, where I met Hines Hines and Dad, a wonderful act.

When I appeared in Buffalo at the Statler Hilton, I couldn't believe my luck when I met and was on the same bill with the crush of my younger years, Nelson Eddy. I used to drive my grandma crazy to go and see whatever movie he was in. Such a handsome guy and what a voice! So when I met him in person I was in seventh heaven. If only my grandma had been alive, I would have shared my thrill with her. He was a lovely person and laughed when I told him of my crush.

From there I sang at the Hotel Syracuse in New York. Then I appeared at the Hilton in Pittsburg, Pennsylvania, when the big baseball game was in town. It was a thrill to meet with Mickey Mantle, Casey Stengel and all those wonderful players, who invited me to dinner. They watched my show and then they invited me to watch their *show*. What a thrill! To this day, my grandson, Willie, is thrilled to have my picture taken with Mickey Mantle in his room.

One of my fondest memories was when I met the lovely Anne Baxter at a friend's home, where she invited me to sing at a party she was giving at her home in Connecticut. We stayed friends until her death of a heart attack on the street in New York City not far from my home. What a loss! She was a wonderful, talented woman. I miss her. Music has always been my *drug*, my wonderful elixir that helped me forget the tragedies and unfairness life often brings.

In 1959, I moved to E. 75th Street to a lovely apartment with trees in the back, a rarity in New York City and a welcoming change from hotel rooms. I continued working and getting good reviews from local newspapers and Variety magazine. I managed to get some bookings by myself, since some booking agents were more than I could handle, especially those who asked for me to do certain things in exchange for a job. I would just walk away along with many other acts.

Charley Peterson was one of the decent ones. My spectacular gowns were made by an Italian woman, whose name was Mabel and many actresses were her clients. I sometimes had a problem with American rhythm, so I had my orchestration made with that problem in mind to cover it.

Again years went by until 1962, when I met Willy Michelin who was to become my second husband. Until that time, I had some unimportant flings, but then I met Willy who had moved into one of the apartments in my building. My landlord introduced us. He was an Austrian engineer who had recently moved to New York and had a brother living in New Jersey. He was a respectable man, hard working, and with a great job. At 43 years old, he had never married. For the first time in a long time, I fell in love again. We were married in 1963 and I was truly happy. I slowed down on my booking engagements and Willy came with me whenever possible. During our first year together, we went to Austria and France to meet our families. He was very proud of my achievements, but being from the mountains of Austria, could not understand why it took me an hour to put on my makeup before going on stage, which I found amusing. He was a handsome man with the most beautiful blue eyes I had ever seen.

During the war, he had been requisitioned against his will, to fight on a German U-boat. Only a very few came back, but he was one of the lucky ones. We had a few good years together and traveled a lot, mostly to the Caribbean, which he loved. However, he had a temper and drank much too much. His war experiences had left him with deep psychological scars, but he was a good man.

We then decided to bring Leslie Anne and Stephen back home, something I had wanted for a long time. Brian had served in Vietnam as a Green Beret, which made me very proud. He had become a handsome man, the spitting image of his father. The children were finally back with us and we made plans to bring them, including Brian, to Bonaire (Dutch Island). Everything went fine until one day Willy drank too much and went swimming. After two hours, he was still missing. I was sick with worry.

The children reproached me and said I worried more about Willy than I did about them. Sometimes you can't win. Finally, Willy reappeared. He had been swimming among sharks, stingrays and other creepy creatures for over two and a half hours.

Not long after that vacation, we all went to St. Croix, except Brian, who could not join us. Again, a wonderful beginning was followed by Willy's drinking too many rum punches, accompanied by beers, so he became loud and nasty. We were at the airport's restaurant waiting for a flight to Martinique. Leslie refused to eat the food he had ordered, which sent him into a rage. He then made a very loud scene and left, leaving us stranded at the airport, so our plane came and went. We were the only three passengers left at the airport until late that evening. I asked a worker on his way home to please call the police, which he did. The Chief of Police arrived with his deputy, two very nice black men, who were shocked finding the three of us in that situation. The chief, George Washington (his real name), took us in our rental car to the jail and sent his deputy out looking for Willy. It was a *charming* jail, surrounded by coconut trees, chickens and roosters. We were offered to sleep in the jail or we could sleep in our car—I chose the car. After a most uncomfortable night, the three of us woke up with the sound of "cock-a-doodle-do." The chief came and told us Willy had been found, snoring on the beach. George Washing gave him a tongue-lashing and told him that what he did was not only nasty but very dangerous, but he could have been attacked by thieves. Leaving his family stranded was irreprehensible. The chief was warm and friendly, so I made a generous donation for his help, for which he was very grateful. It took two days before Willy and I spoke again. Another incident about food and Leslie happened again, but this time in St. Thomas. Willy was a good person except for his drinking, which became constant.

I decided to try a day job and keep away from show business for a while. By then, the Big Bands and Cabaret singers (chanteuse) were cooling, being replaced by different sounds of entertainers like Elvis Presley and the Beatles.

As in my younger days, I became a secretary, this time for Air France in the Legal Department. Willy was pleased, but mostly for the discount tickets, which I received for our personal travel. However, bureaucracy was never my bag, so I couldn't wait to go back to show business.

During my first Christmas party at Air France, I met Tony Giunta, who was to play a great part in my life. He worked at Air France Cargo in JFK. Like me, he loved music and played drums for many years in France. He was born in France of Sicilian parents who emigrated from Sicily and his father became a miner. Someone had introduced us because of our love for music. I had noticed him at that party while he was dancing, since he was a wonderful dancer and could have been a professional. He told me later that he had noticed me and wanted to ask me to dance, but I was surrounded by all the Air France 'big shots.' We became friends.

I contacted the Director of Air France and told him that my musicians and I would be willing to put on a show for any Air France parties. My offer was well received, so I signed a wonderful accordionist, Michel Freiberg, and gave our trio a name, JJ and the Primes. I asked Tony to be the drummer and, later on, I added a great Argentinean guitarist, Rodolfe Alchiron, to our trio. So once again, I was a singer, but this time with a band of my own.

I remember when I first started in show business, I had to fight creepy talent agents, who only would give you a job, if you would *audition* on their office couch. I lost a lot of jobs and so did many other singers. Having my own band was a wonderful change, but I did not know at the time that I was pregnant. When I found out, I had to put my new orchestra and plans on hold. I wasn't feeling at all well, so the doctor ordered me to rest. After four months, I started bleeding and passing heavy clots. I didn't tell Willy, since we were both so happy to have a child. I thought if I stayed in bed, it would be better, but it wasn't. I was 43 years old at this time. One Friday as I lay in bed, the pains became overwhelming. Willy had taken the day off and he and Leslie Anne had gone to the roof to get some sun. I got up, threw a robe on, and dragging myself to the elevator, pushed the fifth floor. However, I still had six steps to climb to get to the roof. On my hands and knees, one step at a time, I made it there just in time to collapse. Luckily, Leslie Anne had heard my calls. Willy and my daughter took me immediately to my doctor. His diagnosis was peritonitis. "Two more days and she would have been dead," the doctor told Willy. I was very ill and stayed in the hospital for over two weeks. The doctor warned me never to get pregnant again. Willy and I were heartbroken. The baby we had lost was a boy. Having children for us now was out of the question.

I tried to divert my heartache by spending much too much money and Willy by drinking even more. He became very quarrelsome and verbally abusive. I guess it was his own way of coping. The children did not get along with Willy, especially Leslie Anne, who reproached him for being too rough and loud in public especially when drunk. She wanted to go to Austria. So in 1966, she was happy when we sent her to visit Willy's mother for a while. Stephen had gotten a job and moved into his own apartment.

Leslie Anne returned from her visit in Austria and Spain. In 1976, she married a wonderful man, Georges Panaglotis from Ohio. He did very well for himself and his family. They have five children, three boys and two girls.

In 1984, my Uncle Jean, who had visited us the year before, died of cancer of the pancreas, which was a big loss for me. Willy by then had retired. We traveled quite a bit, but our relationship was strained. He decided that we should have a 'temporary' separation. He felt we both needed to take a break from each other. In 1987, he decided to leave and stay in Europe for a while to 'clear his mind.' However, since he hadn't felt well for some time lately, he decided to have a complete checkup before he left. We were quite relieved that everything came back negative. He left promising to be back, whatever his decision.

I continued performing as JJ and the Primes Trio. We were doing quite well. We appeared at the Mercury Hotel in Paris, France. Upon my return to New York, I received a call from Willy. He said that he missed me and had decided to come back within a week to stay. I was overjoyed. Two days later, I broke my ankle.

Before I had left for France, Leslie Anne called to let me know that her father, Eddy, had died of a heart attack. Although I didn't love him, I felt sorry and said, "May God bless him."

Over one week had passed without news from Willy. I started to worry. I did not speak Italian, so I asked my friend, Tony to come to my home and call Willy's cousin in Trieste. It seemed like forever to get the phone to ring in Trieste. Finally, someone answered and Tony asked to speak to Willy. There was a long pause, then I saw Tony's countenance change. Afraid to ask, I stood there trembling. "I'm so sorry," were Tony's first words.

"No, please God, not again!" I pleaded. I knew without being told the terrible words that were to follow. Tony spoke after a long time, choking with each word, "Willy died from cancer of the pancreas two days after he spoke with you." This was the same illness that had also taken my uncle away.

My friends were there to help me and try to lessen my pain, but it was not enough—the pain was too great. Willy had been a good man, but like myself, he had been a product of his time and went through hell and back. He had passed away on June 12, 1988, which was the same day I had broken my ankle. Even though he was away from me at the time, he was on his way back, to be with me. My heart was broken.

One by one, all the people that I had loved in my life had gone; almost like a conspiracy. I was left with an unbelievable pain in my heart. It was a time in my life when I almost gave up. The strength I had always shown had disappeared. After all, I was 64 years old. My career was ending. The music I'd loved had been replaced by new strange loud sounds for which my generation, including myself, had no feelings or love.

My children had their own lives.

However, weakness or feeling sorry for myself was not in my nature, so, when Tony and Marie Louise invited me to come to Florida and visit them, I gratefully accepted. They had built a lovely home in Englewood on a canal. I stayed in a bedroom facing the pool. I was very well received it was there that I fell in love with Florida. They introduced me to the Cultural Center of Port Charlotte where I was asked to sing. I promised to come back. Tony and Marie Louise had been a big help, but after two lovely weeks, I returned to New York. I tried my hand at the French Institution, like FGTO and still did club dates. By then, JJ and the Primes were dissolved, since our accordionist had fallen ill.

Not very long after my trip to Florida, my son, Brian, called me to let me know that his father, Albert Taylor, who had been my first husband, had passed away. He had never remarried. He had been a gentle and decent man who should never have married me. He deserved better. He was 86 years old. May God bless him.

A few years went by and one day in 1998, my good friend, Tony Giunta, who had also been the drummer in our trio, called to let me know that his beloved wife, Marie Louise had passed on. She had an operation on her arteries and didn't come out of it. It was very hard for Tony and their children. She had been a wonderful woman, intelligent and a perfect housewife.

After some time had passed, Tony called me and asked what I thought of leaving New York. He asked me to come to live with him and perhaps start working together again. It sounded like a wonderful idea. I was 78-years-old and Tony was 75. Senior Citizen entertainment! Why not? Tony and I had known each other for a long time. He was a good man with a terrific personality and we got along just fine.

In 2001, he came to New York to help me pack. We were in my apartment on that terrible morning of September 11th. Someone on television announced that a plane had "accidentally" flown into the World Trade Tower, only to be told a few minutes later that another passenger airliner had flown into the other Tower. The realization was sudden and brutal. We had been attacked! Another evil, cowardly attack against innocent human beings, but tragically, this was nothing new in our world, with villains like Hitler being one of the last psychotic murderers, among many.

In the year 2003, I moved in with Tony, a move I have never regretted. I knew that a few years back, he had been operated on for cancer of the colon, from which he had come out fine. In 2004, he was diagnosed with blocking of the arteries, which required six bypasses. Thank God again, for his coming out just fine.

Both of us went back to the Cultural Center of Port Charlotte. Every Monday, they have a show that at that time was organized and directed by LaVerne O'Donnell. She was a lovely widow, who had contracted polio when she was young and was confined to a wheelchair. She liked me and asked me to sing in her show called, *Fun with Music*. Unfortunately, after two years, she became very ill. She then asked me to take over her job, which I accepted with great pride. She passed away on October 5, 2006, with a beautiful funeral and memorial for this very special lady.

We now have an average of ten musicians and double that during the 'Snow Bird Season.' The orchestra is handled by our wonderful and talented pianist, Rosalie Steelwell, while I am in charge of the talent, which is all benevolent in favor of the Cultural Center. There is a small charge to come see the entertainment, so it's a Senior Citizen Heaven. They come to dance and listen to the great old music they love. What a joy it is to watch them dance numbers like the foxtrot, polka, waltz, and rumba. We even have a handsome man of 96, who never misses a dance.

Soon after I became in charge of the show, our drummer, Tom, retired to be near his family, which left the door wide open for Tony. It was almost like old times. Most people had been coming here for years like Shirley and Howard Delong, Vinny and Rose Collica (a very talented couple), Eleanor and Mike Demalto, Bob and Lucy Kenyon, who is a talented woman who does a very entertaining 'Mimike.' We also have a lovely lady, Carmen Ferris, who is a volunteer cashier at our shows, whose husband was an airline captain—a very classy lady. Among our entertainers, I cannot forget Pauline Pasquin and her beautiful voice And her husband, Ernie, who plays the harmonica. To round out our musical team, we have Bernie Ackerman, our talented, handsome keyboard man, and our dear Glenn Lowe, sax player and MC. He loves to make me blush by praising my past and present exploits. Every time before I come to the mike to sing, he introduces me by adding, "The great voice of Jackie from Normandy." His wife, Julie, is a sweetheart. Last, but not least, is dear good-hearted Peggy Bradley, who is not only in love with the microphone, but also loves having her picture taken whenever the occasion presents itself. Peggy and her husband, Joe are very friendly and kind people. Tony was thrilled to be playing the drums again and everyone likes him.

Some of our entertainers sing a bit off-key or forget the lyrics, but that is also part of the fun at our programs.

My very glamorous past is long gone along with my youth, but I love my new life and those dear people at the Cultural Center. Unfortunately, many have passed on since Tony and I started volunteering, but their memories will live on forever in our hearts.

Tony's daughters, Jocelyn Orlando and Micheline Bustamente also live in Englewood. They are very nice girls and we get along just fine. Their husbands, Vincent and Luchow, and their children are like family to me. Tony's daughters are happy to see their father playing drums again.

Tony and I have a strong bond that comes from time and respect. We are from the same generation and went through the same dangerous times. Did I feel for him forty years ago—yes, of course, I did. He was a very sexy man and the kind of man I admire. He is always ready to fulfill his responsibilities, but in return, expects his woman to fulfill hers. We were both married, so we became and stayed very good friends, but now in the twilight of our years, music is our passion. My motto has always been, "Have a lot of friends, but trust only very few!" We have a few very good friends.

My dearest friend, Siri Brancaccio, stayed in my life for

fifty years. We met at the home of a mutual boy friend, Bunty Laurence, with whom we shared more than friendship. He later married a Princess from India. Siri had been a showgirl who, among other famous entertainers, had appeared at the well known Lou Walter's Latin Quarter. Lou Walters was the father of Barbara Walters. Siri had been brought in from Sweden to perform. She married someone to be able to 'legally' stay in the states, which was a common procedure back then, especially among foreign people with long contracts in the U.S.

In November 2006, Siri's nurse called me to let me know that she was very sick. I knew that she had cancer of the lungs. Tony and I had made many trips to her home, which was a 3½ hour drive. For a long time, the doctors had been extracting a black fluid from her lungs, but eventually the time came when nothing more could be done, except morphine. She had always shown such courage. We arrived at her home early one morning and one of the hospice ladies let us in. The once very beautiful girl, whose lovers had been among the most famous names, was painfully thin. Her face, ravaged by pain, lit up when she saw me. As I kissed her cold and damp forehead, she whispered, "Darling Jackie, I am dying you know." I could not answer for the tears were choking me. She slowly took my hand. "Don't cry, Babe," her favorite nickname for me. "God is with me." There was a very long and painful silence. Then in her last attempt to cheer me up, she spoke with only great difficulty. "Do you remember, dear friend, when we were both young and beautiful?" I tried to smile. "Yes, I do, darling Siri, please don't talk anymore." She closed her eyes. "I love you, old friend," were her last words. I sobbed, "And I will always love you, God Bless you."

My last memory of her was with her eyes closed, her hand over her beloved Bible, as if asking for forgiveness. She was never an angel, nor pretended ever having been one. She lived a full life, as I did. We were very much the same, as we both did what we had to do to survive in a man's world and we were both sinners. Siri passed away that same night, November 18, 2005. My darling friend, was now my darling angel.

Among the friends I made at the Cultural Center's *Fun with Music*, is a lady with whom I immediately connected and made friends, Mary Jane De Pillo. She and her husband, Phil, return every winter from up north in Pennsylvania to their Florida home in North Port. Mary Jane is like the sister I would have loved having and I am happy to say, she feels exactly the same about me. Herself no stranger to life's heartbreaks, she recently had lost her beloved daughter to cancer—an unbearable tragedy forever present in her heart. Life can be so cruel. Phil De Pillo has a beautiful voice and could have been a professional. He sings on Mondays at our show to everyone's delight. They both became very good friends and introduced us to Kathie McMann and Steve who also became our friends.

Tony and I took a vacation in 2007 to visit his family in France. We had a great time except for my breathing, which seemed to become increasingly difficult. Upon our return, I decided to see Dr. Clifton Lewis in Sarasota upon our family doctor, Dr. D. Gooding's recommendation.

I was in Dr. Lewis' office with Tony and my daughter when he came in—a very good-looking, imposing man. I could tell by his countenance that something was wrong. "Jackie," he started "your valves have to be replaced."

"My what?" I asked. He explained what they were. "Doctor, can something else be done besides an operation?" He looked at me and slowly shook his head. "Jackie, without an operation, you have six months to live."

Life had prepared me from a very early age for unexpected tragedies, but this one was a beaut! "It stinks," was my answer to him and then I started crying. Doctor Lewis got up, put his arms around me and said, "Come on, Princess, it will be just fine." This was a nickname he had given me after my daughter had proudly spoken to him about my impressive and strange past. He also was trying to cheer me up for what was coming next. "The operation will be done by a robot, which took some time to register. I looked at him in disbelief and finally I gasped, "A what?" "Don't worry, Princess, it will be me and a robot. It is a fairly new procedure." I couldn't help but ask, "Am I your first guinea pig?" "Nope," he answered with a mischievous look on his face, "the robot ate the last one." I couldn't help but laugh, which was just what he had hoped. Besides being a great heart surgeon, he has a great sense of humor and a relaxing bedside manner, which is so important.

All arrangements were made And all the necessary tests were done. Finally June 19, 2008, the date of the operation, arrived.. The hospital was the Greater Sarasota Memorial Hospital and the operation lasted seven hours, but it was a success. One valve was replaced and the other one was fixed with *pig skin*. I was to leave within four to five days, but unfortunately, complications set in of pneumonia and a stomach infection. A tube was inserted into my nose and throat into my stomach for ten days. The first insert went wrong and had to be redone—pretty bad. As I was ready to be transferred to another hospital, another infection set in. Dr. Clifton Lewis came in to see me one last time at the hospital. "Why don't you stop being sick Princess? You're giving me a bad name." Knowing my illness had nothing to do with the brilliant operation he did on my valves, he was there to lift up my spirits with one last professional visit.

"Keep fighting, Princess and you'll do just fine."

I was transferred to the hospital in Punta Gorda. Compared to the Sarasota hospital, I hated it. I was given so many pills that I was over-medicated and completely out of it. One special pill given to me stopped me from eating. I lived on water for a month and a half. I lost forty pounds. My friends kept bringing food to me, which ended up in the garbage, since I had developed a hatred for food. Another pill made me lose all my hair, so I was extremely ill and depressed. I think the love of Leslie Ann, Steve, Brian, Tony, my grandchildren and a great amount of friends is what kept me alive. I guess God didn't want me yet. During my illness, I was moved five different times—from hospitals to nursing homes and visa-versa. They finally discovered the pills that made me stop eating and losing my hair. I went down from almost thirty pills a day to five.

When I finally left the hospital, my first visit was to Dr. Lewis. I needed help to walk. The Doctor was happy to see me. No one thought I'd come out of it. As it was, it took me three months to return home. I developed melancholia and couldn't stop crying, but Dr. Lewis still had not lost his sense of humor. When I complained about the pain in my right 'boob', which they had to go into during the operation, he said, "Stop playing with it." Tony, Leslie Anne and I were still laughing as we left his office. Laughter is sometimes the best medicine. The operation on my valves had been successful.

In all sincerity, I don't know how I came out of it alive. I was known to hate pills, so the nurse was told to stay with me until I swallowed all of them. Yuk!

Unfortunately, a few days later, Dr. Lewis told his patients that he was returning to Alabama, which was a terrible loss for Sarasota and Florida. He is a great surgeon, and I might add with mischief, had I been young, he would have been my choice. God Bless Him.

Sometimes mothers and daughters don't get along very well, which is not my case. When I was ill, Leslie Anne took exceptional care of me and was at the hospital every day with Tony. An altogether 2½ hour drive for Tony, because my daughter doesn't drive so Tony picked her up and then took her back to her home. I am also deeply grateful to my friends for their kind visits, cards and phone calls.

My position at *Fun with Music* was put on hold until my return. My friends, Rosalie, Carmen and Pauline handled it in my absence. Three and a half months later and fifty pounds lighter, I returned to our show. As I was called to the microphone and started singing "Because of You," I received a standing ovation. Not for my voice, which had lost its power, but from sheer happiness to see me back from another of my 'near death experiences.' Such friendship is a gift from God and I started crying out of gratitude and love for these very special, wonderful people who seemed to erase all the evil I had encountered earlier in my life.

My strength, of course, was very slow in coming back, but then what can be expected at my age? As months went by, more medical interventions were needed, including shingles and gall bladder. I am 85 and learning to live with constant pain.

I am grateful for my life, both the good and the bad. Regrets? I have many, mostly for the people I have deeply hurt and for putting love before reason. Also, I should have been a more understanding mother, but not for the lack of loving my children. There are some very private matters that I will take to my grave to protect the ones I loved, as well as not embarrass them. I am very proud of my two beloved countries: France and the United States. God love and protect them always.

would like to proudly acknowledge some of the famous people I was lucky to meet and/or work with:

Mickey Mantel, Casey Stengel, and Sammy Davis, Jr.

George Jessel, Anne Baxter, and Sessue Hayakawa

Liberace, Barbara Nichols, and Hoagy Carmichael

Nelson Eddy, Edith Piaf, Jackie Gleason and John Verona

Rudy Valle, Ed Sullivan, Milton Berle and Tony Bennett

Gary Morton, Alec Guinness, Peggy Lee and Bob Hope

Rita Hayworth, Hines, Hines and Dad, and Bobby Darrin

Harold Lloyd, Jr., Billy Eckstein, Julia Skouras

and Nelson Rockefeller

Photo Gallery

The
PERSIAN
TERRACE
HOTEL
SYRACUSE
SPECIAL
ATTRACTION
Songs in 5
languages by
JACQUELINE
JOURDAN
Charming, talented
and oh, so French!
TED HUSTON
AND HIS ORCHESTRA
APPEARING TUESDAYS THRU
SATURDAYS THRU FEB. 17
DINNER:
6 to 9 p.m.
No couvert,
no minimum
SUPPER:
9 p.m. to 1 a.m.
Couvert: Sat. $1.50
Tues. thru Fri.
No couvert,
Minimum:
Tues. thru Fri. $1.50
Saturday $2.50
Reservations:
Call HA 2-5121

OO! La! La!
PARIS
comes to
PITTSBURGH
when
Jacqueline Jourdan sings
for supper dancing nightly in the
KING'S GARDEN
with the ART LOWRY TRIO
no cover • no minimum—from 9 till closing
The Pittsburgh Hilton

The Rendezvous Presents

Dick Wilson

"His Fabulous Violin"
and His Orchestra

Delightful arrangements for your
dancing enjoyment

Featuring

Jacqueline Jourdan

The Provocative Parisienne

And continuous dancing
Saturday night with

Tone Carnevale's Trio

also . . .

The Arthur Murray Champagne Interlude

featuring a special dance contest Friday evenings at 10:30 p.m.

Drexelbrook
DATE LINES
VOLUME 1, NUMBER 6
AUGUST, 1961
JACQUELINE JOURDAN
MONDAY, AUGUST 14
LOUIS ARMSTRONG
MONDAY, AUGUST 21
WOODY HERMAN
MONDAY, AUGUST 28
The TOMMY DORSEY ORCHESTRA
Featuring WARREN COVINGTON
plus
Drexelbrook's Own BIG BAND
Led by TOMMY FERGUSON

Jacqueline Jourdan is the singing star appearing in the Ritz Cafe of the Ritz-Carlton Hotel.

Le Pavillon

Elegant Parisian atmosphere in the LaSalle Hotel. Dancing nightly except Sunday. Open 11.00 a.m. to 12.00 p.m. Fri. and Sat. to 1.00 a.m. Sunday to 10.30. Cold Buffet à la carte Sunday.

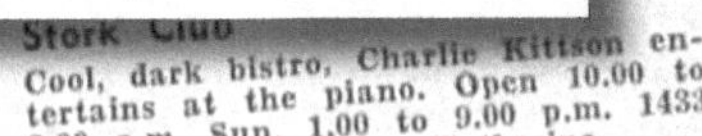

Stork Club
Cool, dark bistro, Charlie Kittson entertains at the piano. Open 10.00 to 3.00 a.m. Sun. 1.00 to 9.00 p.m. 1433

June 9, 1962
Week

SHERATON-BLACKSTONE

where to go
what to do
when in Chicago

The sultry French singer, Jacqueline Jourdan, whose spirited warbling has set night club audiences of three continents to shouting "Vive La France," appears in the Cafe Bonaparte of the Sheraton-Blackstone through June 16

Maurice Sey

EL Embassy Club

Música Bailable desde las

PRESENTA
A
JACQUELINE
JOURDAN
Cantante Internacional
Intérprete en diferentes
Idiomas
Y ADEMAS
NEREIDA
y
MIRITO
Bailarines Acrobáticos
Dominicanos
Shows a las 10:30 p.m.
Maestro de Ceremonias
GRULLON CORDERO
Música Bailable desde las
9:00 p.m.
AGUSTIN MERCIER

Jacqueline ("Don't Call Me a Chantoosey") Jourdan, sultry French singer, who has set plush night club audiences of three continents to shouting "Vive La France" will open in the ....(dates) .... it was announced today by .. ..(manager.

Jackie, who loves life and sings that way, has recently returned from a successful tour of South America and has starred at Chicago's famed Cafe Bonaparte at the Sheraton-Blackstone; Shamrock Hilton Hotel in Houston; Ritz Carlton, Montreal; Pittsburgh Hilton; and Old New Orleans, Washington, D. C.

The delightful Jackie has hit the jackpot on the European cabaret circuits and is a classic style Parisian night club triller in the best Right Bank tradition.

"Chantoosey," claims this good natured canary, is a cynical word, too often denoting a singer who is French but can't sing. Although Jackie doesn't approve of the word "chantoosey", she can't buck the lure of alliteration which impels critics to endow her with the title of "Choosy Chantoosey"not only because of her high calibre repertoire but also because this girl with a figure like Brigid Bardot is still unmarried.

An exceptionally charming girl with a pleasant, friendly manner, and good eye for the spectacular in gowns, she appeals to the analytical in the ladies With her chic and her natural good looks hold male attention. She is"a lot of woman." She approaches her audience in a cheerful mood and conveys her good spirits to her listeners. She also uses the traveling microphone technique to good effect. With this she reaches individual tables and gives a song or two the personalized treatment.

SHERATON-BLACKSTONE HOTEL •   MICHIGAN AVENUE at BALBO • CHICAGO • HArrison 7-4300

Newsletter

HOTEL INTER·CONTINENTAL CURAÇAO

Dear Guest:

We would like to extend to you our most cordial welcome to the Inter-Continental Curacao and at the same time we would like to acquaint you with some of the facilities we have for your enjoyment.

DUTCH HOUSE COFFEE SHOP. Commanding a dramatic view of the harbour entrance, this charming Coffee Shop is located on the first floor and is open from early breakfast to late   supper.

KINI KINI BAR. Completely redecorated, this cool oasis is located on the first floor, just opposite the elevator. Indulge in convivial conversation while sipping long and leisurely (or short and snappy) drinks in a comfortable Country Club atmosphere. Open from 11. 00 A. M. on.

WATERFORT ROTISSERIE. This elegant and sophisticated restaurant is also located on the first floor. Try the top choice steaks and chops from the Charcoal Grill, succulent slices of roast prime ribs or, if you are in the mood for continental cookery, take Shashlik Caucacien or Fondue Bourguigogne. This warm, intimate, brick and beamed Rotisserie overlooking the pool terrace also offers seafood from the surrounding seas as well as Keshy Yena and Stoba - classic cuisine of Curacao. Our wine selection is unexcelled. There are two seatings for dinner: 7. 00 to 9. 00 and 9. 30 to 11. 30. FOR RESERVATIONS PLEASE CALL THE MAITRE D'HOTEL OR THE RECEPTION DESK.

LA CAVE DE NEPTUNE. Snug hide-a-way built within the arches of Curacao's 150 year old Waterfort. Swinging rhythms nightly with HERNANDO AND HIS COLOMBIAN ORCHESTRA in the Caribbean's most unique nightclub with Peek-A-Boo peering through the swimming pool portholes. - Open from 9. 00 P. M. until late hours. In this unusual set-up a truly exciting show is opening tonight. It is one which we are sure you will enjoy, featuring:

JACQUELINE JOURDAN

This famous singer will perform for you every night until Sunday, April 20. The show will take place at 11. 00 P. M. with the exception of Saturday when the first show will be at 10. 00 P. M. and second show at 12. 00 midnight. FOR RESERVATIONS PLEASE CALL THE MAITRE D'HOTEL OR THE RECEPTION DESK.

We wish you an enjoyable stay.

THE MANAGEMENT   14/4/69